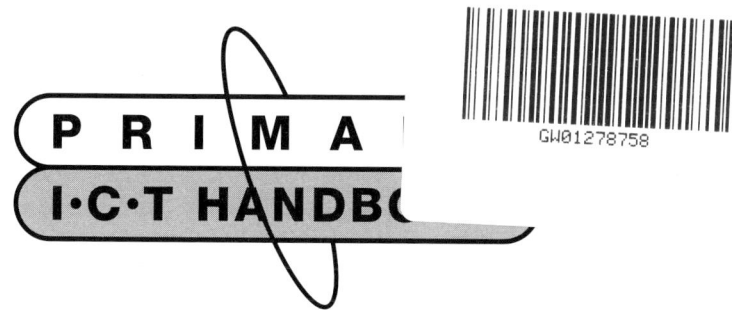

Science

THIS BOOK BELONGS TO MISS DIXON

Chris Drage

Text © Chris Drage 2001
Original illustrations © Nelson Thornes 2001

The right of Chris Drage to be identified as the author of this work has been asserted by him in accordance with the Copyright, Designs and Patents Act 1988.

All rights reserved. No part of this publication may be reproduced or transmitted in any form or by any means, electronic or mechanical, including photocopy, recording or any information storage and retrieval system, without permission in writing from the publisher or under licence from the Copyright Licensing Agency Limited, of 90 Tottenham Court Road, London W1T 4LP.

Any person who commits any unauthorised act in relation to this publication may be liable to criminal prosecution and civil claims for damages.

Published in 2001 by:
Nelson Thornes Ltd
Delta Place
27 Bath Road
CHELTENHAM
GL53 7TH
United Kingdom

01 02 03 04 05 / 10 9 8 7 6 5 4 3 2 1

A catalogue record for this book is available from the British Library

ISBN 0 7487 3727 8

Page make-up by Florence Production Ltd.

Printed and bound in Great Britain by T.J. International Ltd.

Acknowledgements
Screen shots: 'Biology at Key Stage 1' designed and programmed by Gaynor Perry; 'Me' designed and programmed by Keith Wass; Music Games – © Inclusive Technology Ltd; © 1998 E. Bate (Soft Teach 01985 840329); Flowol software, © Keep IT Easy from Data Harvest.
All other screen shots produced with the kind permission of Granada Learning Ltd.

Contents

Introduction 1

Classroom organisation 7

Management of ICT 10

Resources 18

ICT resources checklist 24

Science software resources 25

Science links in the DfEE
QCA ICT Scheme of Work 30

5-14 National Guidelines for Scotland 31

Key Stage 1/P1–3 activities 32

Key stage 2/P4–7 activities 48

Glossary 76

Introduction ▼

With two out of every three jobs in Europe requiring some degree of skill in Information Communications Technology (ICT), the modern education system avoids effective delivery of ICT at its peril. However, despite such statistics, according to a survey by the British Educational Suppliers Association (BESA, *ICT in UK State Schools Survey*, 1999) only about 45% of primary school teachers feel confident and competent with ICT, learning their ICT skills as they go along and keeping just one step ahead of their pupils. Yet ICT is an integral part of the modern curriculum, one which crosses the boundaries of all other subject areas both in terms of the support it can offer and as a context for teaching IT skills.

▼ Why use ICT in science?

ICT can really bring science to life, capturing, illustrating and analysing data in many different situations. Taking data capture as an example, the computer can take the drudgery out of having to collect and record measurements. Pupils can set up the equipment, which will then take the readings for them, and any changes can be seen immediately as they occur.

For years it has been said that in primary schools pupils spend far too much time producing graphs rather than interpreting them. Using computers:

- graphs can be produced instantly, leaving pupils more time for interpretation;
- a variety of graph types can be produced, sometimes revealing different aspects of the data and allowing pupils to choose which representation is appropriate to a particular set of readings;
- by putting a formula into a spreadsheet, a degree of modelling can take place, and those 'What if' questions can be answered. For example, upper KS2/P4–7 pupils who are studying energy might study the food energy levels in a pizza. They could have a target of a particular energy value to be met by choosing from a variety of toppings. If the spreadsheet has been set up with each topping's energy value, entering various toppings on the spreadsheet will calculate instantly the total energy value for that pizza. Thus pupils can conduct an investigation which otherwise would be virtually impossible due to mathematical and time restraints;
- pupils can record, display and share their work using word processing and/or desktop publishing packages;
- any pictures taken on a digital camera or scanned from a photograph can be added to complete the topic;
- CD-ROM and Internet-based information can be searched for background material or to gain additional knowledge.

ICT can be used effectively to support and enhance pupils' learning in science and to help to develop their ICT capability at the same time. The ICT curriculum strands are the processes whereby pupils will develop their overall ICT capability; and they outline the specific areas required and what types of software should be used. In science these are, briefly:

Communication ▼

- word processing
- desktop publishing
- drawing programs
- painting programs
- multimedia authoring programs

➡ 1

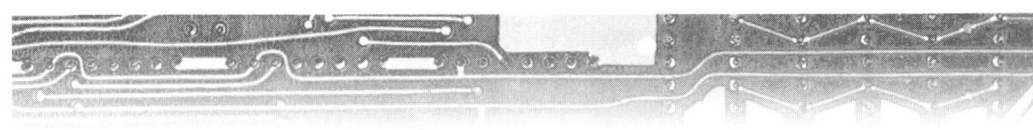

▶ Science processes/skills

Recording and presenting information in an appropriate manner using tables, bar charts and line graphs to present results

Information handling ▼

- databases
- hierarchical databases
- graph plotting programs
- CD-ROM materials

▶ Science processes/skills

- deciding what data should be collected
- making observations and measurements
- storing and retrieving information
- making comparisons and identifying trends or patterns in results

Monitoring ▼

- sensor reading and data-logging programs

▶ Science processes/skills

- considering what apparatus to use
- using apparatus appropriately and correctly
- collecting and displaying environmental and experimental data

Modelling ▼

- simulations
- spreadsheets

▶ Science processes/skills

- using results to see patterns and to draw conclusions
- changing one element/variable and observing the result

▼ National Curriculum 2000

For the first time, a rationale has been included as an introduction to the National Curriculum. This sets out the aims and values of the school curriculum and the main purposes of a national framework. These are:

- to establish an entitlement;
- to establish standards;
- to promote continuity and coherence;
- to promote public understanding.

There are general teaching requirements on inclusion, use of language, use of ICT and health and safety. A new statutory statement on providing effective learning opportunities for all pupils replaces the current statutory statements on access. The new statement sets out three key principles for inclusion:

- setting suitable learning challenges;
- responding to pupils' diverse learning needs;
- overcoming potential barriers to learning and assessment for individuals and groups of pupils.

Schools need to take action at all levels of curriculum planning to ensure that individual requirements are met. The science orders set out the knowledge, skills and understanding to be taught and the breadth of study in terms of content, context or experiences.

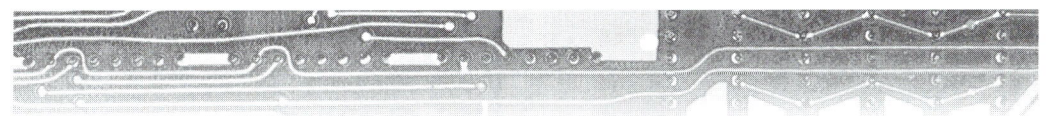

The National Curriculum, at least, places the onus on teachers not only to deliver the subject, but also to deliver it in a way that embraces today's technology. ICT is not and need not be the province of the specialist teacher. The classroom computer has helped us:

- to discover new ways to facilitate the learning process;
- to include areas of learning new to the curriculum;
- perhaps more importantly, to offer access to the curriculum to some pupils whom traditional methods have excluded.

Without good software, however, the school computer is about as useful as a cassette recorder without tapes. It is important to regard the computer as a resource to be integrated within the curriculum and not as an object in its own right. This may not be enough to convince you, however, if you are nervous of technology and have not yet got to grips with computers.

Each school needs to create:

- a structure in which computer materials can be used across the curriculum;
- a system whereby staff can communicate their computer experiences to their colleagues;
- and an atmosphere where all teachers understand the possibilities offered by computers to enhance pupils' learning and are willing to 'have a go' themselves. It is only by adopting a positive attitude that teachers will facilitate the success of computing in school.

Therefore, each school needs to develop:

- an ICT policy that is a working document;
- an ICT curriculum map;
- a scheme of work in ICT;
- a working environment where colleagues are encouraged to share their experiences and are prepared to learn from each other.

OFSTED inspection reports highlight some of the problems inherent in the broad assumptions made above. For example:

- ICT is being marginalised due to other pressures and a lack of teacher expertise;
- there is little teaching that will help pupils progress beyond their existing levels of attainment;
- the development and support of pupils' ICT capability depends on the commitment and expertise of too few staff in schools;
- the needs of such staff when teaching and assessing ICT are rarely met.

The reasons for this situation are many. Not least is the problem of technology moving ahead faster than schools and teachers can cope with. The matter of teacher confidence in ICT is a key issue. For only when teachers are confident users of ICT themselves, will the payoff come for the pupils. Cross-curricular use of ICT will only work when teachers are confident in ICT, where pupils' progress is monitored, and when structures are in place for motivating and effectively co-ordinating delivery. Each school must formulate its own strategies.

It is beyond the scope of this guide to offer assistance except in relation to science. However, there are documents from both Becta and QCA which will assist in formulating an ICT policy and a scheme of work, which also give examples of standards and their monitoring.

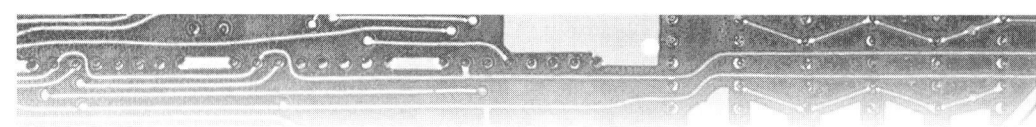

▼ Planning for ICT

It is the aim of this guide to provide a practical framework for a scheme of work in ICT from KS1 to the end of KS2.

The following table is a reference guide indicating where ICT fits into the programme of work for science.

KS1	KS2
ICT Statutory Requirements **SCIENTIFIC ENQUIRY** **2g** **Statutory:** pupils should be taught to communicate what happened in a variety of ways, including using **ICT** **BREADTH OF STUDY** **1c** **Statutory:** pupils should be taught the knowledge, skills and understanding through using a range of sources of information and data, including **ICT- based** sources	**ICT Statutory Requirements** **SCIENTIFIC ENQUIRY** **2f** **Statutory:** pupils should be taught to make systematic observations and measurements, including the use of **ICT** for data-logging **2h** **Statutory:** pupils should be taught to use a wide range of methods, including diagrams, drawings, … and **ICT**, to communicate data in an appropriate and systematic manner **BREADTH OF STUDY** **1c** **Statutory:** pupils should be taught the knowledge, skills and understanding through using a range of sources of information and data, including **ICT-based** sources
ICT Opportunities, Examples and Links **SCIENTIFIC ENQUIRY** **2g** **Statutory:** pupils should be taught to communicate what happened in a variety of ways, including using **ICT** **ICT link:** this requirement builds on ICT/3	**ICT Opportunities, Examples and Links** **SCIENTIFIC ENQUIRY** **2f** **Statutory:** pupils should be taught to make systematic observations and measurements, including the use of **ICT** for data-logging **ICT link:** this requirement builds upon ICT/2b

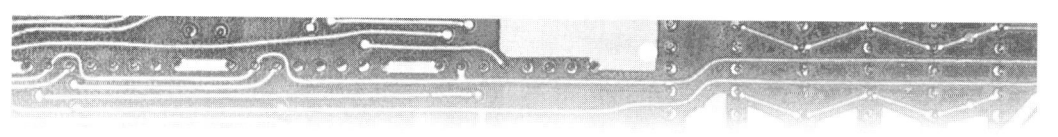

LIFE PROCESSES AND LIVING THINGS

2a
Statutory: pupils should be taught to recognise and compare the main external parts of the bodies of humans and other animals
ICT opportunity: pupils could use multimedia sources to make comparisons

4a and b
Statutory: pupils should be taught to recognise similarities and differences between themselves and others, and to treat others with sensitivity, and to group living things according to easily observable similarities and differences
ICT opportunity: pupils could use data collected to compile a class database

MATERIALS AND THEIR PROPERTIES

1b
Statutory: pupils should be taught to sort objects into groups on the basis of simple material properties
ICT opportunity: pupils could use a software package to combine words and pictures about materials and objects

PHYSICAL PROCESSES

3c
Statutory: pupils should be taught that there are many kinds of sound and sources of sound
ICT opportunity: pupils could use sensors to detect and compare sounds

2h
Statutory: pupils should be taught to use a wide range of methods, including diagrams, drawings, ... and **ICT**, to communicate data in an appropriate and systematic manner
ICT link: this requirement builds on ICT/3

LIFE PROCESSES AND LIVING THINGS

2b
Statutory: pupils should be taught about the need for food for activity and growth, and about the importance of an adequate and varied diet for health
ICT opportunity: pupils could use a database or spreadsheet to analyse data about types of food in school lunches

2c
Statutory: pupils should be taught that the heart acts as a pump to circulate the blood through vessels around the body, including through the lungs
ICT opportunity: pupils could use video or CD-ROM to see things that cannot be directly observed

2e
Statutory: pupils should be taught that humans and some other animals have skeletons and muscles to support and protect their bodies and to help them to move
ICT opportunity: pupils could use video or CD-ROM to see things that cannot be directly observed

2f
Statutory: pupils should be taught about the main stages of the human life cycle
ICT opportunity: pupils could use video or CD-ROM to see things that cannot be directly observed

4a
Statutory: pupils should be taught to make and use keys
ICT opportunity: pupils could use a branching database to develop and use keys

5

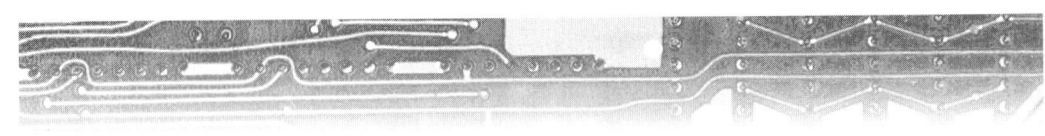

KS2 continued

5b
Statutory: pupils should be taught about the different plants and animals found in different habitats
ICT opportunity: pupils could use video or CD-ROM to compare non-local habitats

5f
Statutory: pupils should be taught that micro-organisms are living organisms that are often too small to be seen, and that they may be beneficial or harmful
ICT opportunity: pupils could use simulation software to show changes in the populations of micro-organisms in different conditions

MATERIALS AND THEIR PROPERTIES

2b
Statutory: pupils should be taught to describe changes that occur when materials are heated or cooled
ICT opportunity: pupils could use sensors to record temperature changes

2e
Statutory: pupils should be taught the part played by evaporation and condensation in the water cycle
ICT opportunity: pupils could use CD-ROM or the Internet to research water supplies in a range of localities

PHYSICAL PROCESSES

1a
Statutory: pupils should be taught to construct circuits, incorporating a battery or power supply and a range of switches, to make electrical devices work
ICT opportunity: pupils could use simulation software to extend an investigation of components in a series circuit

3f
Statutory: pupils should be taught how to change the pitch and loudness of sounds produced by some vibrating objects
ICT opportunity: pupils could use sensors to detect and compare sounds made under different conditions

4b
Statutory: pupils should be taught how the position of the Sun appears to change during the day, and how shadows change as this happens
ICT opportunity: pupils could use video or CD-ROM to study models of the Sun, Earth and Moon system

4c
Statutory: pupils should be taught how day and night are related to the spin of the Earth on its own axis
ICT opportunity: pupils could use video or CD-ROM to study models of the Sun, Earth and Moon system

4d
Statutory: pupils should be taught that the Earth orbits the Sun once each year, and that the Moon takes approximately 28 days to orbit the Earth
ICT opportunity: pupils could use video or CD-ROM to study models of the Sun, Earth and Moon system

Classroom organisation

There are a number of management issues which relate to the successful use of the classroom computer. Good classroom organisation contributes greatly to success with the computer and also helps to minimise technical problems.

For some teachers the organisation of the computer into the everyday routine of the classroom presents many difficulties, not least of which is the simple fact that, more often than not, there is only one. The computer may be regarded as just something else that has to be planned for and for many a reluctant user it is a real problem. It is easy for all to understand that the computer should be used – indeed the ICT National Curriculum demands that all pupils have access to this technology – but for some the computer is an intimidating piece of machinery. Without the appropriate knowledge, these teachers may well be convinced that the computer and printer never function correctly when they use them.

Teachers may say they do not use the computer for the following reasons:

- it is disruptive;
- they want programs that the pupils can use without a teacher (the computer is regarded as a teaching machine for drill and practice);
- there is no time for the computer;
- time spent on other subjects is more important.

▼ Building confidence

The issue here is really one of self-confidence. In enabling these teachers to move from a position of reluctance and fear to one of confidence and conviction, the following strategies may be worth some consideration:

- Limit the amount of software to just a few programs. The aim is to get to know these well.
- Install the software onto the hard disk first if possible, keeping copies of the floppy disk or CDs as masters.
- Learn how to load, save and print from the program.
- Where appropriate, introduce the program to the whole class to ensure a common understanding and starting point.
- Provide some help cards for the program.
- Make a few rules for the class such as:
  - use the help cards;
  - ask at least two other pupils for help before asking the teacher.
- Plan the use of the program as part of a project or topic.
- Plan when the computer will be used and by whom, and how much support will be available.
- Ensure that the computer, printer and chosen program are all working together correctly before the pupils start work.
- Set aside some time to discuss with the pupils what they have done (a whole-class discussion may be a valuable way of developing expertise).
- Encourage pupils to save their work regularly, especially before printing (if the printer does not work it may cause the computer to freeze and the only way to unfreeze the computer is to switch it off, thus losing work).

▼ Pupils as independent computer users

Independence means responsibility and pupils can be taught how to:

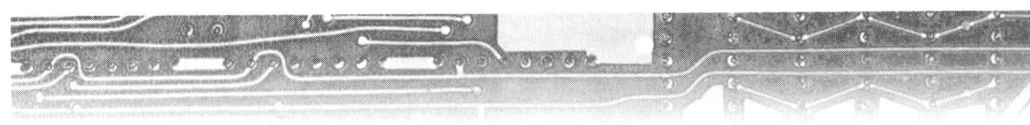

- handle disks carefully and be responsible for them;
- start and quit the program;
- save and print their work;
- load the printer with paper;
- handle floppy disks and CD-ROMs correctly;
- shut down and switch off the computer;
- share their expertise with other pupils.

▼ Grouping the pupils

Three pupils in a group working at the computer often seems to offer the best organisation. The make-up of groups may vary and will depend on the nature of the task. Observe the groups from time to time to ensure that all the pupils are sharing the activity and that one or two do not dominate.

▼ Positioning the computer

The siting of the computer system is of immediate importance. Most classrooms were built before the computer was invented and they are frequently not ideal places for computer use. Some considerations follow.

- It is best to make the position as permanent as security will permit, keeping the computer system as far away from the white- or blackboard as possible.
- Ideally, the computer should be placed away from bright light to avoid reflection on the screen. Reflections not only make the screen difficult to read, but also detract from concentration on the work at hand.
- Similarly, it is important that the screen does not face the rest of the class; pupils working at the computer do not then feel that they must protect their work from onlookers and nor, in turn, are the rest of the class distracted.
- Having the computer near the carpet helps when introducing a new program to the whole class, giving them somewhere comfortable to sit as a group.
- Although it is tempting to enclose the computer table with bookshelves and screens, adequate space must be retained for pupils to sit comfortably and for their notebooks, plans, maps, help cards and other materials. Restricting the space around the computer also makes it very awkward to reload the printer with paper or to do any other technical adjustments.
- All mains cables should be placed out of the way and it is advisable to use a multipoint socket with its own on/off switch. If you can afford one which isolates the system from the effects of power surge, so much the better. It is wiser to provide sockets for future peripherals like a control box or overlay keyboard.
- EC Directives on computer use, coupled with the problems that can arise in accommodating new systems, highlight many shortcomings and compromises across the school which the acquisition of modern furniture would help eliminate. In a primary school it is important to site the stand-alone machine correctly so that the best use may be made of it.
- As computer use frequently means a group activity, enough space must be available for a group of three pupils to sit comfortably around the screen. Older pupils may need space for a control/sensing interface box and models.
- In primary schools a computer is often a shared resource or must be moved around the teaching/learning area. A trolley should be chosen with rubber wheels at least

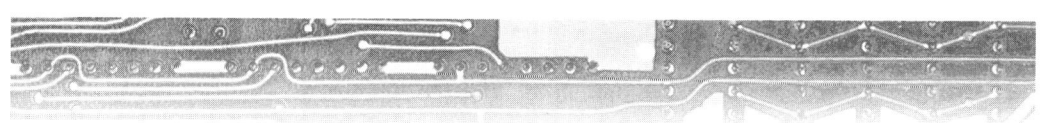

75 mm in diameter, two of which incorporate brakes. The trolley should be able to fit through a standard 650 mm doorway but also conform to the 800 mm depth necessary to comply with the EC VDU directive. To meet these two demands, the worktop must slide out to its working position and be able to retract safely before being moved. For stand-alone systems like multimedia computers in a library or learning resource area, large mobile trolley workstations are more appropriate.

Standard computer furniture will not be appropriate for wheelchair or standing frame users. The answer here is to provide a suitable type of adjustable furniture which can cope with infinite variations in height. Similarly, with the visually impaired or those who have restricted mobility and co-ordination, a variety of input devices may be needed (e.g. switches, overlay keyboard, tracker ball). A larger workstation is called for to accommodate these extra items safely.

No matter where or whom you teach, there must be an agreed, co-ordinated action plan for ICT so that new computer systems, peripherals and furniture all combine successfully.

from ten minutes to a few hours to complete a piece of work, depending on the type of activity. It is most difficult to assess the time required to complete a given task when using word-processing and desktop publishing (DTP) programs. Initially, pupils might use the word processor for short tasks, such as writing headings and labels for topics and displays, and move on to writing reports about a science experiment, rather than immediately trying to write a long and complicated story.

▼ Time management

The management of time poses the biggest problem by far. It is vital that the teacher be familiar with the software and time must be found for this to happen. This is important so that the teacher may make an estimate of how long each group might need to complete a task. The amount of time a group needs at the computer really depends on the type of software being used. Pupils may need anything

Management of ICT ▼

▼ Tasks, roles and responsibilities

The role and responsibilities of the ICT co-ordinator are increasingly complex. Although there are many 'standard' areas which all schools will expect to be the responsibility of the ICT co-ordinator, there are others which might belong to the senior management team or the science co-ordinator.

The science co-ordinator's role ▼

A science co-ordinator is expected to provide professional leadership that leads to high-quality teaching, effective use of resources and improved standards of achievement. It is vital that the science co-ordinator ensure that pupils are given opportunities to develop and apply their information technology capability in their study of science. This requires that:

- scientific understanding is enhanced by appropriate use of ICT;
- learning of science is enhanced by ICT;
- ICT skills are enhanced by their application to science;
- pupils are given appropriate opportunities to use ICT to collect, store, retrieve and present scientific information;
- there should be appropriate progression from being able to use ICT to judging when to use ICT to collect, handle and investigate scientific information.

As information and communication technologies develop further, teachers and pupils need opportunities to use these technologies in appropriate ways to fulfil the aims of science education. For example, teachers should be able to evaluate the potential of video-conferencing, e-mail communication and Internet access as tools for learning.

More generally, the school should offer support for teachers' attempts to bring ICT into the science curriculum. This requires recognition that ICT facilities are as essential as magnets and microscopes, and that teachers may require additional training in the effective implementation of ICT in science.

The ICT co-ordinator's role ▼

Do not be surprised, if you are ICT co-ordinator, when other staff interpret your role quite differently from you. In particular, you may find that your view of your role differs from that of the senior management team who appoint and manage you and oversee your work. It may also differ from the view of other staff who are on the receiving end of your efforts to co-ordinate ICT.

The effective delivery of ICT capability must necessarily be shared with other colleagues, so it is important to ensure that responsibilities are known and understood clearly by all parties.

▼ Writing an ICT policy

Writing the introduction ▼

Who is the intended audience for the policy?

- members of staff
- parents and the local community
- external agencies and organisations

What should the policy achieve?

- ensure all staff understand and agree on the approach to ICT
- assist planning and promote development

The ICT Co-ordinator ▼

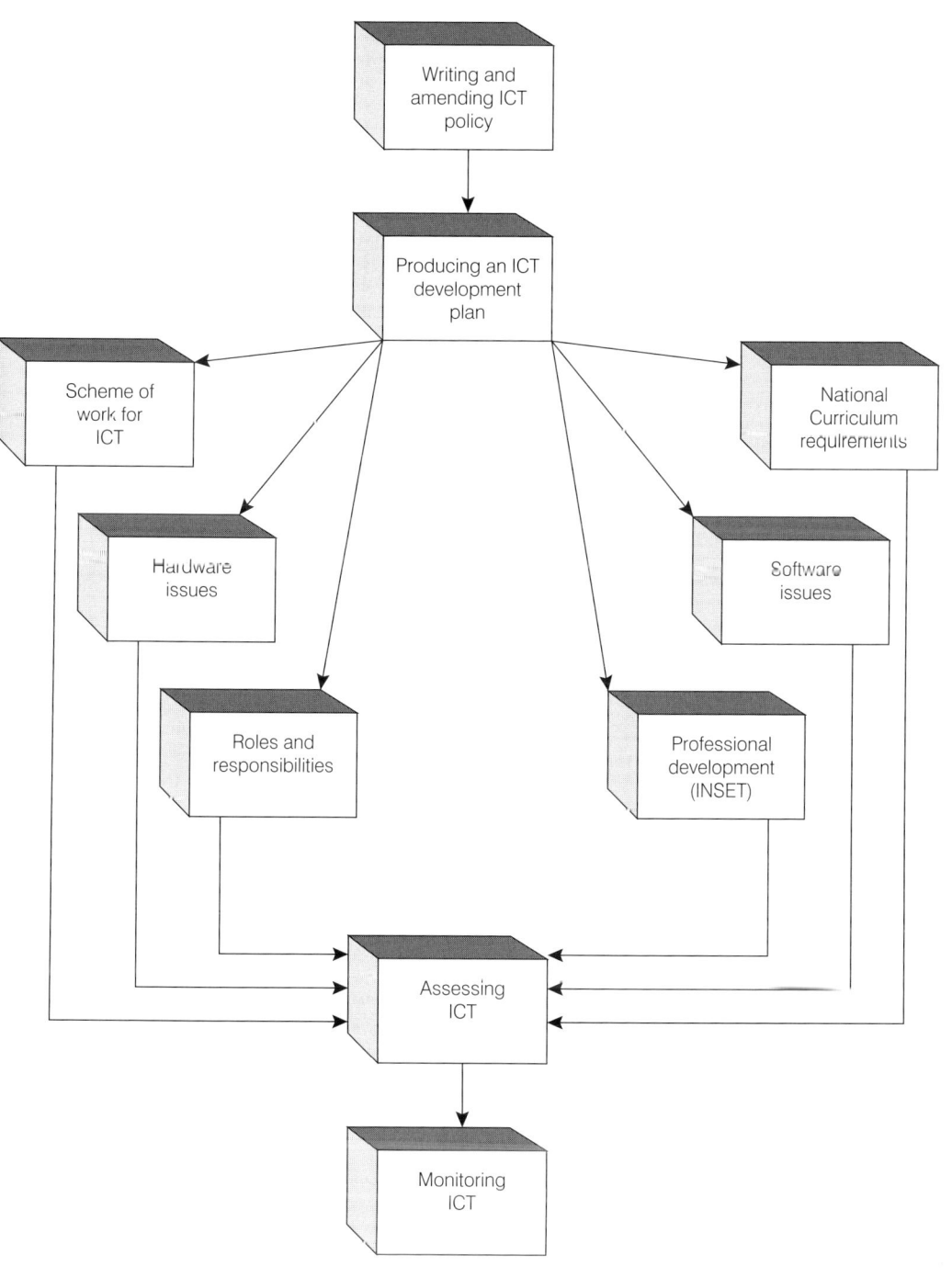

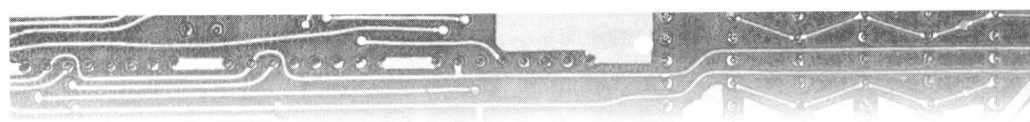

- explain the school's position to outsiders
- assist the governors in the allocation of funds

What are the other policy issues?

- When was the policy developed?
- Who was involved?
- Which other documents need to be cross-referenced?
- Is the ICT policy linked to the School Development Plan?
- What does 'Information Communications Technology' cover?

What do you consider to be part of ICT?

- computers
- inclusive technology, for example overlay keyboards
- voice-operated equipment
- programmable toys
- calculators
- pressure pads
- temperature sensors and probes
- light sensors
- electronic musical instruments
- audio and video recorders

- digital cameras
- scanners

What are the other considerations?

- Do you wish ICT as used in school management/administration to be covered?
- How will assessment information be handled?
- How will support be provided?

The school's curriculum organisation ▼

- How will the school deliver the National Curriculum ICT requirements?
- How is ICT capability developed through other subjects?
- Is ICT capability developed through topic-based work?
- How is differentiation planned?
- How does ICT support and enrich learning across the curriculum?
- How does ICT contribute to cross-curricular themes?

The school's aims ▼

Table 1

Influential factors to be considered when writing your aims for ICT

Internal factors	Local factors	National factors
the school's general aims	LEA targets	National Curriculum requirements
your School Development Plan	school partnerships	OFSTED (for example, feedback from inspection)
special features of your curriculum	intake characteristics	national training targets
strengths and interests of staff	support available, for example, special needs	

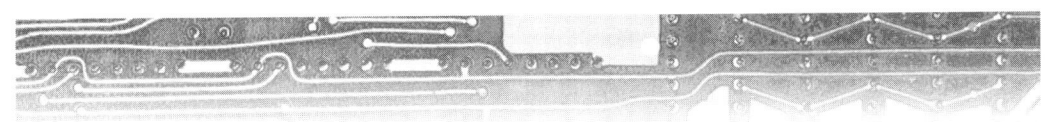

Roles and responsibilities ▼

You should state the roles and responsibilities of key areas of ICT in your school:

Table 2

Involvement and responsibilities of people involved in developing ICT in your school

Some of the people involved	Some responsibilities to be allocated

governors
deputy head
head teacher
senior managers
ICT co-ordinator
classroom teachers
subject co-ordinators
special needs co-ordinator
assistants and adults other than teachers
parents
pupils
	ensuring:
	   – the consistent implementation of ICT policy
	   – staff access to ICT and identifying support needed
	   – continuity between year groups
	   – ICT progression
	liaison with feeder and/or receiving schools
	purchasing/organising ICT resources
	arranging in-service support
	reviewing the ICT poilicy
	assessment of pupils
	meeting statutory requirements
	curriculum development
	overseeing equipment maintenance
	health and safety policy and practice

Teaching and learning styles ▼

- What learning styles are you able to support?
- What teaching styles do you encourage?
- How do you differentiate between learners and ensure that they are all challenged?

Access to ICT ▼

How is ICT equipment deployed in school?

- class-based computers
- computer clusters
- networked computers
- portable computers
- printing facilities
- other peripherals (scanners, alternative keyboards etc.)
- control and data-logging equipment

What are the other issues?

- Do you make provision for pupils to use ICT equipment outside lessons?
- Are pupils able to use ICT equipment unsupervised?
- Do you have open-access areas such as the library?

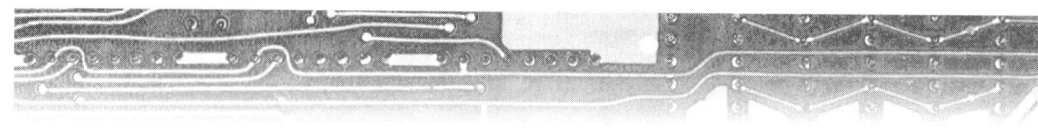

- Is there a loan scheme for portable equipment?

Equal opportunities ▼

- How do you ensure that all pupils have opportunities to use ICT according to their needs?
- How does ICT help to give pupils with special educational needs access to the whole curriculum?
- How does ICT support more able pupils?
- How do you take account of gender issues?
- How do you take account of pupils' access to ICT at home?

Recording, assessment and reporting ▼

- How does practice with ICT reflect the school's policy on recording, assessment and reporting?
- What additional demands do you take into account?
- Do you keep a school portfolio of work in ICT?
- Do you have an agreed format for record keeping?
- What mechanisms are there for moderated assessments – 'agreement trialling'?
- How much evidence of individual ICT work is kept and for how long?

Managing resources ▼

How is the budget for ICT resources determined?

- annually on a formula basis
- through negotiation with staff each year
- as part of a medium-term plan
- long-term budgetary arrangements to meet new and emerging concerns

How is the deployment of hardware determined?

- through discussion with staff
- according to a development plan

How are software resources identified, acquired, updated and deployed?

- through discussion with staff each year
- through audits and reviews

How do you ensure that all staff have the appropriate skills to use ICT resources effectively?

- skills audits and appraisal
- staff loan of equipment
- continual professional development training programme

What external services do you use to support ICT in the work of the school?

- curriculum support
- technical support

Monitoring and review ▼

How do you monitor:

- current practice to ensure that the existing policy is implemented?
- ICT teaching?
- planning?
- marking?
- ICT use?

What are the review issues?

- How are schemes of work reviewed and developed?
- How are staff development needs identified?
- How, when and by whom will the ICT policy be reviewed?

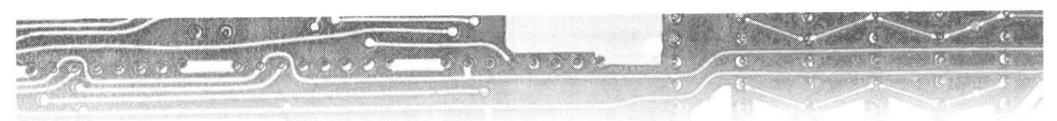

▼ Preparing an ICT development plan

You are most likely to be asked to produce a three-year development plan for ICT. You will need to consider the following:

- the plan should be more than a list of the hardware you want to buy over the next few years;
- you must remember that the whole-school development plan will probably contain issues that will have an impact on ICT;
- your plan should outline a staff development programme for ICT;
- developments will need to be planned for each key stage.

The hardware audit ▼

In addition to listing all your equipment, it is essential that you also include some idea of its age, although this need not be too accurate. There may be nobody in your school who can remember when a particular computer was acquired, so a 'best guess' will suffice.

To help with calculations later, the easiest way to record age is to show when a particular device was bought new. Bear in mind that this may not be when the school obtained it. Where this is the case, you will need to estimate its original year of purchase. To make a complete hardware audit easier, we will start with probably the most important component, namely the school's computers. We can carry out a similar procedure later for all the other hardware resources such as printers, overlay keyboards, control equipment, floor robots etc.

You need to create a table, entering the number of computers to show the year when they were bought new. A useful task at this stage (if you have no other handy record) is to enter serial numbers for all computers (and monitors) so that if any are stolen they will be easier to trace. You should create a subtotal column that shows the quantities of computers by type and a subtotals row that shows the quantities of computers in the year they were new.

A further task at this stage might be to make a note of where all your hardware is normally kept and used. This can be done very efficiently on a simple school plan with the main computers shown graphically, and can prove useful when you are thinking strategically about where to locate equipment in the future.

Using the information contained in the audit form, it is very easy to see an age profile for your school's computers. This can be particularly enlightening if your school has a large number of old computers! You can now use the information in the age profile to prepare a replacement plan.

Once older equipment is withdrawn from use, numbers obviously fall unless that equipment is also replaced. A good replacement plan does not necessarily mean that you should just throw away older computers. Curriculum demands may mean that you invest in new computers with extra features such as CD-ROM drives, but the older computers may still have a valid use elsewhere in the school, and may allow you to declare an even older machine to be obsolete.

Software issues ▼

Most primary schools have adopted the idea of a common set of software – a 'toolbox' – which is used throughout the school. Quite apart from the economic value of being able to purchase multi-user licences for software rather than a single-user licence for every

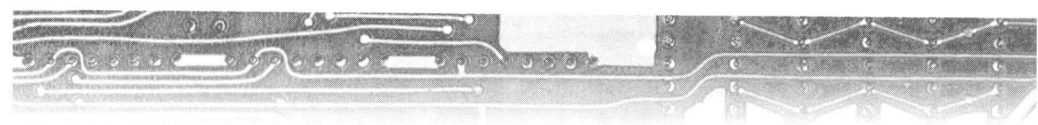

computer, this also makes more flexible use of resources.

It also means that both teachers and pupils can develop and transfer their ICT skills; for example, they do not have to learn to use a different word processor each year. Subject-specific software may be used in addition to the basic toolbox of software, in order to develop subject knowledge (see the section on science software resources). It pays to keep the list as simple as possible. It is also advisable to involve others in compiling the list, as it will be easier for other teachers to see why some programs are suitable for certain ages only and why they need to be replaced to increase the level of ICT attainment.

▼ Staff development

- Plan to support teachers before they will need to use a particular ICT aspect or skill in their scheme of work.
- If you have just put a new item of hardware on the list of requirements, now is the time to plan for its support.
- Prioritise those areas of the schemes of work that are weakest among staff, but most urgent in the plan.

▼ Assessment of ICT

Since the Dearing Report, the programmes of study have been the basis for planning, teaching and day-to-day assessment. All of the Programmes of Study for ICT must be taught throughout the key stages, but there is no requirement to assess every part of them.

It is important to decide which parts to assess on a regular basis so that staff can decide which of the level descriptors gives the best judgement at the end of the key stage.

The other reason for making assessments is to make sure that pupils are making progress and developing their ICT capability in a systematic way.

The very least that is needed is a plan for how assessment will be developed in your school. You may already have this on your ICT development plan. It will give those who need to know the timescale for assessment in ICT and the markers along the way. The way to thrive is to carry out your plan. Make sure that any action to be carried out by you is transferred to your individual action plan. Any action involving funding or staff meeting time will need to be raised with the appropriate person, well in advance. If your planning has been shared with senior managers at the outset, it should be easier to get agreement when necessary.

Possible monitoring strategies include:

- looking at teachers' planning for ICT each term and checking levels from learning outcomes;
- talking informally with teachers about what they are teaching the pupils in ICT;
- using a staff meeting to look at samples of work and agree levels – this works well if done whilst developing a strand of ICT for a scheme of work;
- discussing the level descriptors to develop understanding of what we expect of pupils at each age.

Assessing attainment ▼

The range of levels within which the majority of pupils are expected to work are:

- KS1 (levels 1–3): majority of pupils expected to attain level 2
- KS2 (levels 2–5): majority of pupils expected to attain level 4

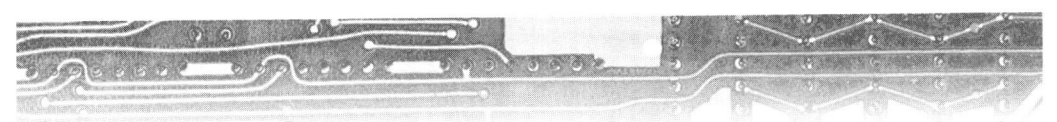

In deciding on a pupil's level of attainment at the end of a key stage, you should judge which description best fits the pupil's performance and consider this alongside descriptions for adjacent levels. The level descriptions in the National Curriculum document list aspects of attainment, based on the programmes of study, which are needed to build up a picture of a pupil's performance over time in a range of contexts. Similarly, the level descriptions can help to determine the degree of challenge and progression for work across each year of a key stage and can also be used as a basis to describe pupils' progress when reporting to parents

▼ Professional development

Without continuing professional development, little progress is possible. As they get to grips with the use of ICT in the classroom, teachers tend to go through a number of stages which may be characterised as familiarity, experimentation, adoption and integration. Supporting colleagues through these stages of development requires different forms of intervention.

For many teachers the first hurdle is the greatest. All sorts of fears combine: 'What will happen if I break it?'; 'Will I make a fool of myself?'; and 'The kids know more than I do.' These are just a few of the more common ones. A bad experience at this stage can produce permanent damage, so you need to tread carefully. I have found that friendly one-to-one help after school can go a long way. A good introduction will focus on an application that teachers can quickly translate into classroom practice. Be aware too that switching on and making the machine work is the easy bit – incorporating ICT into teaching and learning is a far greater challenge which needs careful planning.

Running INSET ▼

A well-planned and organised Professional Development Day can make a real difference in moving ICT forward in your school. Two key factors tend to constrain the successful use of these days: expertise and resources both need to be considered beforehand. If you choose a centre other than your own school, check that:

- it is equipped with computers and other resources that match those in your school;
- the centre staff work with you in agreeing the objectives and content and will adapt to meet the needs of your colleagues;
- there are opportunities to assess different approaches and to try out equipment and software that you might later purchase

If you want an external trainer to run an event in your school, make sure they are prepared to visit and assess the situation first. Again, you will want to satisfy yourself that they can supply what you need rather than what they think you ought to have.

You also need to consider who will attend and whether you should include classroom assistants, nursery nurses and senior management as well as classroom teachers.

Opportunities to reflect and plan are another essential ingredient. Courses sometimes concentrate entirely on the acquisition of software skills and do not provide opportunities for colleagues to relate the software skills that they acquire to the classroom activities that they will support. A minimum aim ought to be that everyone decides on at least one learning activity that they will try with pupils in the classroom.

Resources

While the activities are designed to be as flexible as possible, certain minimum resources are essential requirements. These include:

▼ Hardware resources

It is essential that pupils have regular access to computers with printers, which may be regrouped in clusters or on a network. Similarly, it is essential that there is access to colour printers, a scanner or digital camera with associated software, a multimedia computer, and data-logger.

▼ Local area networks

Local area networks (LANs) offer a range of benefits to learning, deployment and management of resources:

Benefits to learning ▼

LANs can provide access to a wide variety of in-house education services and applications. Teachers, lecturers and pupils can communicate with each other electronically, sending messages, exchanging resources and working collaboratively, wherever they are located. In addition, the provision of an Internet connection at every workstation means that the children can access a wide range of external services. These services might be provided nationally via public websites, via subscription services, or via restricted services such as might be provided by an LEA to its educational establishments.

Benefits to deployment ▼

LANs enable peripherals and resources such as printers and CD-ROMs to be shared. They also facilitate file sharing, so that information is more widely accessible. Data and resources can also be backed up centrally, so that security is increased.

Benefits to management ▼

A LAN can help to reduce bureaucracy, by helping to automate and simplify a wide range of school administrative tasks. Teachers can gain access to the school's LAN from anywhere in the school for record-keeping and the preparation of reports. Governors too can communicate electronically with the school and staff, distributing information via the network and thus saving time and reducing paperwork.

However, purchasing ICT is complex, time-consuming and requires technical expertise. Selecting the correct ICT package for an institution from the large number of potential service providers is a difficult process, particularly when value for money is a high priority. Installing and maintaining a network is also a specialised process, calling for a high level of technical expertise. The answer here lies in managed services.

The National Grid for Learning Certified Managed Services (CMS) aim to support management in all these areas, by defining a service which meets the needs of each particular school. This ensures that Certified Service Providers have reached a benchmark of minimum standards; institutions can compare whether the equipment and services on offer meet or exceed the minimum standard of provision and can be confident about their quality. Similarly, CMS ensure that Certified Service Providers deliver and commission all equipment, software and services to the satisfaction of the institution, and also offer appropriate training in the use and administration of the networks and services

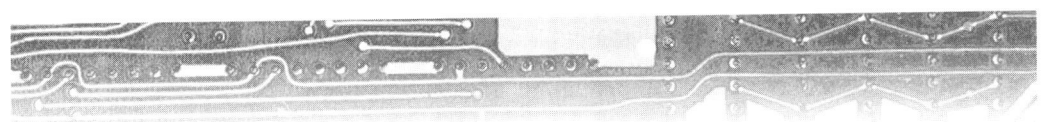

provided. This helps enormously, as there is a single point of contact for advice, supply and support. Part and parcel of the service is a predictable and manageable charging structure to assist schools in financial planning.

Equipment

Data-logging ▼

Data collection and sensing in science are still not well delivered in primary schools. This is not surprising when you consider the need for interface boxes, leads, sensors, software and of course the need to get the computer as close to the centre of the investigation as possible. Then there is the problem of getting 30-plus pupils through the activity as well.

To date, the EcoLog system (Data Harvest) is possibly the neatest and most elegant solution to taking measurements in science investigations for KS2/P4–7 pupils. Central to the system is the interface box, which takes up little more space than an audio cassette. Other elements include a lead, *Sensing Science Primary* software, and a photocopiable Curriculum Notes book. Powered by one AA battery, EcoLog works quite independently of a computer, only needing the latter for downloading and displaying the data. This means that you can leave EcoLog at any location you want to monitor and let it collect data. EcoLog has three built-in sensors, which means it can measure air temperature, ambient light and sound level. EcoLog Plus goes further by including humidity and pressure sensors. However, to use the system to best advantage you need to use discrete sensors. EcoLog can take two external sensors that are available via Data Harvest's Plug-in Sensor pack. Data-logging is controlled via a single RUN switch which starts/stops/pauses logging.

Sensing Science Primary software has evolved over the years to the point where it is nothing short of excellent. Using its Exploring Section, live data can be displayed as a change of colour, as swing on a dial, as a bar on a chart, or as a numeral. In Snapshot Mode it takes readings from all available sensors, storing them on a spreadsheet-style table where changes over time can be studied. The software also offers a line graph with some interesting features, including the ability to draw predictions on screen and then see what the data actually did. A separate program, GraphPlus, displays data in real time, opening up possibilities for the exploration of environmental factors and how they interact. The package is rounded off with a book containing teachers' notes and work sheets.

Digital cameras ▼

The camera has rapidly become another essential item in the teacher's educational toolkit. This is mainly due to the growing movement in recent years for accountability and the demand that teachers must be able to produce evidence of everything in the classroom. Therefore, although it is impossible to store many of the items pupils design and make in technology lessons, it is a different matter when you photograph their work. In addition to this, a camera has many uses in school, from recording activities and events to celebrating achievement. The cost of it all can become prohibitive, especially when those unavoidable ruined shots are taken into account.

Digital pictures provide evidence of pupils' work for the records and can accompany a display of their work. The LCD colour screen on many cameras enables the photographer to monitor the results of each shot and to take

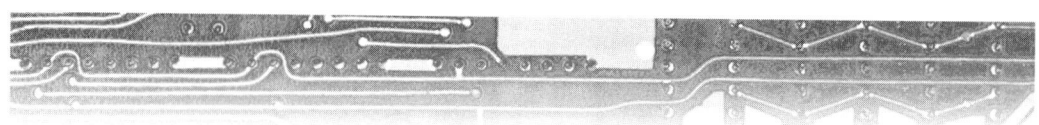

other pictures if necessary. Once transferred to the school's PC the pictures can be sharpened a little, dropped into a DTP document, given a caption and printed out directly on the school's colour printer.

Before you even begin to transfer a single shot to the computer, you do need a machine with a fast processor and at least 8 Mb of memory, preferably 10 Mb, in order to process and edit images efficiently. Nothing is more frustrating, especially for pupils, than having to wait ages for the computer to 'do something'.

Taking a good digital image is no different from taking a picture with an optical 35 mm camera and the same rules for good picture-taking apply. The difference is that there is no film, the images being stored in the camera's memory. The software provided permits images to be viewed as thumbnails which resemble slides. Selecting all or some of the thumbnails and dragging the selection onto a directory on the hard disk downloads the full images and saves them. The exceptions to this are Sony Digital Mavica® cameras, whose images are stored in the form of JPEGs (compressed images) and saved directly onto floppy disks, which is very convenient for school use.

A digital microscope such as the IntelPlay QX3 (TAG Learning) will also be useful as it offers the ability to save images and video clips for use in pupils' written work.

Scanner ▼

A scanner is a device that allows printed documents (photographs, hand-drawn diagrams or text) to be imported into a computer. A scanner is to a computer what a photocopier is to a piece of paper: it produces a copy of the item in memory. You can remove the black spots where there were staple holes, enlarge or reduce the image, lighten or darken it etc. In particular, you can remove dark backgrounds that prevent readable copies.

Depending on the choice of scanner and associated software, line drawings, photographs and text can be 'read' by a computer, in either black and white, greyscale, or full colour. Commonly, scanners are used to import illustrations or photographs into a word processor or DTP program. The computer provides editing and manipulation facilities, eliminating the need to paste images physically into the text whilst maintaining the original in pristine condition. Material can also be inserted into on-line documents such as multimedia presentations, World Wide Web pages and hypertext documents. A scanner, then, is basically a graphic device, generating a file containing an image of the scanned document. However, by use of optical character recognition (OCR) software, a computer can be made to 'read' any text in that image and convert it into 'editable' text. So, if the image is of a printed page of text, OCR allows that text to be read into a word processor, with considerable savings in time over re-keying.

Arguably a flatbed scanner will prove to be the most versatile type for a school, as it allows you to scan photos, paper documents, books, magazines, large maps, or even three-dimensional objects (those that do not have a lot of depth, for example coins).

The scan head and light source – located below the glass – automatically move down the document at a constant speed. Most low-cost flatbed scanners are designed to take A4 sheets, although A3 models are also available. Most measure approximately 400 × 300 × 100 mm, are quite sturdy, and have covers which hinge or adjust to allow you to scan bulky objects. 100 dpi (dots per inch) is

usually quite sufficient resolution for most needs, as software can enlarge small images considerably, although with some loss of quality.
To capture a scan, proceed as follows:

- Place the item to be copied face down on the scanner's glass bed and close the lid.
- Switch on the scanner's power switch.
- Start the scanner software by clicking on the icon – it will generally say something like 'acquire and export' which will prompt you for a file name.
- The next step is to obtain a preview of the image, that is, a small version on which you can frame the part you want to scan.
- Once the preview image is on screen a black frame appears with handles which allow you to move and re-size it to section off all or some of the image for scanning.
- From the toolbar, select the required scanning resolution (usually 100–150 dpi) and the file format in which you want the resulting image (for example JPEG).
- Click on 'scan' and watch the image appear on screen.
- If you are not happy at any time the scan can usually be interrupted, a new preview obtained and the frame re-adjusted
- The final image can either be saved to a file or printed directly.

▼ Software resources

- *My World 2*, or *My World3* and *My World of Science* (all SEMERC)
- *Clicker 4* (Crick Software)
- *Pages* (SEMERC) or *TextEase Studio* (Softease)
- *Dazzle Plus* (SEMERC) or similar paint and vector graphics software
- Clip art files
- *Compose World* (SEMERC) or similar music composition program
- *Pictogram 2* (Kudlian Soft), *Graph Plot* (SEMERC) or similar program capable of drawing a variety of graphs
- *Junior Pinpoint* (Logotron) or similar database management software
- *Granada Branch* (Granada Learning) or similar branching database
- *DataSweet* (Kudlian Soft) or similar spreadsheet
- *Screen Turtle V2* (Topologika) or similar turtle graphics program
- *Control Insight* (Logotron) or similar control software
- Simulations

A range of CD-ROMs include buttons for navigation, hypertext links and the facility to search using keywords, indexes and menus. Most topics will be enhanced by access to the Internet and e-mail.

▼ What is a spreadsheet?

A spreadsheet is a two-dimensional grid of numbers, laid out in rows and columns. The on-screen page may show all, or just part, of the sheet; each location is described as a cell.

Once you have entered numbers into the cells you can carry out certain operations. For example, the spreadsheet can add up the contents of a column of cells and arrive at a total. At a more sophisticated level, you can link a number in one cell to those in other cells by the use of appropriate formulae. For example, a formula might involve specifying a sequence of operations to add the contents of two cells together and put the result in a third cell. You could end up with an automatic large-scale calculator, with quite a number of

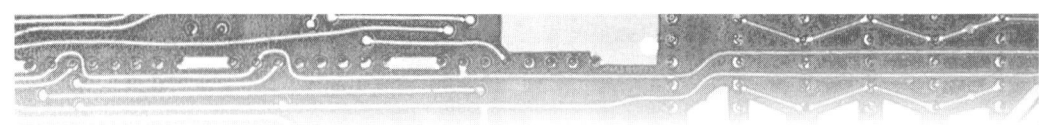

formulae linking different cells together. Hence if the number in a particular cell is altered, this will cause changes to be made to all the other cells that relate to it. If you had a spreadsheet to calculate the monthly outgoings for your household, and then the price of milk went up, you could enter the new price and the spreadsheet would calculate the new daily, weekly and monthly total, the new total food bill, and the new total for outgoings – after just one alteration!

A spreadsheet is particularly useful for replicating the same operation over several rows or columns. In addition, a spreadsheet can do many of the things a database can do. Most have search and sort functions as well as a wide range of graphical displays.

▼ What can I do with a spreadsheet?

A spreadsheet can support any kind of activity in which it is likely that calculations will be carried out upon numbers. Thus, you could use a spreadsheet, for example, to plan a school or class educational visit. A suitable model could be set up to include such things as cost of transport, cost of meals, entrance costs etc, with one column containing a suitable formula to calculate the charge per pupil. Any changes in costs would be reflected immediately in the charge-per-pupil cell. You could explore the effect of different transport quotes or entertainment options without having to rewrite anything.

However, the collection and manipulation of data, the formulation of a hypothesis and discussion of the results form only one application of a spreadsheet. Other applications include modelling, investigations, number patterns and problem solving. The spreadsheet is probably the best all-purpose mathematical tool currently available. Although there is a relatively long learning curve before complete mastery, you can make a start at whatever level you wish. You may use a spreadsheet to produce a range of graphs, or you may start by using the built-in functions to calculate totals, averages and standard deviations.

If you are using an activity in which operations need to be replicated, you can only use a spreadsheet. In other activities it might not make much difference whether you use a spreadsheet or a database, as they do similar things. They both allow you to store a great quantity of data; they allow you to sort data and to find individual records; and they have various options for displaying data using a variety of graphs and charts. Some spreadsheets can be used as effectively as databases in statistical investigations.

▼ Using spreadsheets in the classroom

If pupils are to see the potential applications for spreadsheets, they need to use them over a number of years. They need to start in a modest way; they may begin by using the spreadsheet as a graph drawing tool, without using it for calculation purposes. It is an extremely quick and efficient tool for accepting data and displaying it in graphical format.

As they gain confidence, they may begin to play and experiment with numbers, because calculations can be carried out with ease.

The use of the spreadsheet can give structure to abstract ideas. You can help the pupils to use a spreadsheet as a problem-solving tool, applying standard strategies such as breaking a problem down into manageable bits. The use of a spreadsheet can shift the emphasis from number crunching to

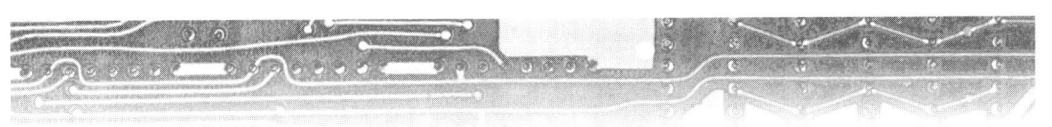

hypothesising, and it can set a real context for algebra. Spreadsheets offer pupils untold opportunities for mathematical discovery and for developing skills relating to:

- investigations involving the collection, analysis, interpretation and presentation of data in order to test a hypothesis;
- the construction of mathematical models;
- investigations into number patterns and sequences;
- solving problems.

The Science National Curriculum makes specific mention of the use of spreadsheets at KS2:

'Sc2/2b Pupils could use a database or spreadsheet to analyse data about types of food in school lunches.'

▼ Databases

Databases may be used for three main purposes in the classroom:

- as tools for helping pupils to become effective information handlers;
- as means of actively supporting the role of concrete experience in learning;
- as information sources to support pupils' subject and project work.

Three main types of information handling systems are used in the classroom:

- view databases store information on pages and can be thought of as 'electronic books';
- hierarchical databases are based on a binary-tree structure, which is a line of information that branches out from a main heading into a number of subheadings, and so on down the tree;
- random access databases are arguably the most useful of all. Information may be extracted from these by asking questions that impose conditions. For example, a database on weather has information stored under different headings (fields) such as cloud cover, temperature, rainfall. To investigate the information, one might ask the computer to find all of the records where 'temperature is GREATER THAN 20 degrees AND rainfall is LESS THAN 20 mm'. The computer would then search through the data file and display the records where these two conditions are met.

The principle of the database concept is that it is not only the interrogation of information in the database that is valuable, but also the collection, organisation and presentation of data; this enables pupils to see the value of information as a resource.

In the first instance pupils will learn to use the classroom computer to find information related to their particular needs. In so doing they will begin to become independent information retrievers.

In the second instance, if pupils are allowed to create databases themselves as part of their project work, they are likely to develop a much wider understanding of how databases may be used to handle information.

The educational value of any database lies in the deductions which pupils may be led to make, based on the implications that rapid 'intelligent' searches of their own collected data make clear. It cannot be over-emphasised that the real learning in database work happens away from the computer: the need for careful consideration of the questionnaire; the discussion of which units of measurement to use; the drawing of tentative conclusions which then need to be tested.

➡ 23

ICT resources checklist

Resource	Activity age	Links to DfEE QCA Science
KS1		
Floor robot e.g. Roamer (Valiant Technology)	YR-2	1A, 1E, 2E
Clicker 4 (Crick Software)	YR-1	1C
Word processor	Y1	1C
Sequences (Granada Learning)	YR	information handling
My World 2, or *My World 3* and *My World of Science* (SEMERC)	YR-2	1A, 2A, 2F
Smudge the Scientist (Storm Educational Software)	Y1	1B
Paint software	Y1	1D
Music composition	Y1	1F
Garden Wildlife (Anglia Multimedia)	Y2	2B
Pictogram software	Y2	2C
Simple database	Y2	2D
KS2		
Internet access	Y3/Y6	3A, 6F
Spreadsheet	Y3-4/6	3B, 4D, 6C, 6D
Data-logger e.g. EcoLog (Data Harvest)	Y3-6	3C, 3F, 4C, 5D, 5F, 6A
Database	Y3-5	3E, 4B, 5A, 5E
Branching database	Y3	3D
CD-ROM encyclopedia	Y3/6	4A, 5C, 6B
Creepy Crawlies (Cumana)	Y4	4B
Floor robot e.g. Roamer (Valiant Technology)	Y4	4E
Simulation software e.g. *Simple Circuits* (Soft Teach Educational)	Y4/6	4F, 6G
Multimedia software	Y5	5B
Control software/kit	Y6	6E

Science software resources ▼

This section lists software including that which does not appear elsewhere in this handbook but which will support learning in science; the list represents some of the best titles currently available. Up-to-date reviews on the latest software can be found on the Nelson Thornes website: www.nelsonthornes.com

▼ Integrated software tools

► KS 1–2/P 1–7

Granada Toolkit (Granada Learning) – PC
This suite of software tools is thoroughly recommended for the applications described in this handbook. They represent a complete core of ICT tools which integrate very well with one another and comprise:

Granada Writer:	word processor
Granada Colours:	art program
Granada Database:	data handling program
Granada Spreadsheet:	spreadsheet
Internet Odyssey 2:	research tool
Toolkit Launcher:	configuration tool

Also recommended is *Granada Branch*, a hierarchical (branching) database.

▼ Life processes and living things

► KS 1/P1–3

Living and Growing (Inclusive Technology) – Mac/PC
A special needs program where pupils match, sort and click on plants, animals or the body to find out about them.

On the Farm (Inclusive Technology) – PC
A special needs disk which centres on a farmyard 'fuzzy felt' activity on which pupils put animal pictures, hear words and sounds, and add labels.

► KS 1–2/P1–7

Becoming a Human Body Explorer (Dorling Kindersley) – PC CD-ROM
Introduction to human anatomy. Pupils take an interactive journey through the body's metamorphoses from child to adult, examining its mechanics and maintenance.

Learn About series (Sunburst) – Mac
There are various titles in the series: Animals, Dinosaurs, Human Body, Insects, Plants, Night Sky. Useful and cost-effective.

► KS 2/P4–7

3D Dinosaur Hunter (Dorling Kindersley) – Mac/PC CD-ROM
This is really a home education title featuring a walk-through virtual museum which pupils seem to relate to well. The CD links to a website where the subject is broadened with stories about new excavations, dinosaur gossip, and a place to ask questions of dinosaur experts. A good reason to get connected!

BodyMapper (TAG Learning) – Acorn/Mac/PC
Where *BodyMapper* scores over other body system software is that it offers a built-in database where pupils can add their personal measurements and plot the results on graphs. This is a useful and practical rather than a glamorous program.

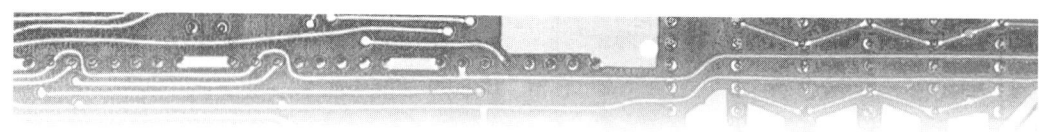

Encyclopedia of Nature 2.0 (Dorling Kindersley) – PC CD-ROM
Describes in compelling detail the rich diversity of life on Earth. Clearly organised into thematic sections, the CD covers a wide range of topics from reproduction and movement to photosynthesis and communication. It explores each major plant and animal group.

Garden Wildlife (Anglia Multimedia) – Acorn/Mac/PC CD-ROM
The town with its attendant cinema, library, park and pond is the scenario in this CD. You can easily find your way to information for about 100 typical garden creatures. No speech in this one, but a solid title none the less.

Growing Up Together 1 & 2 (Granada Learning) – Acorn/PC CD-ROM
This CD is designed for personal and social education covering such topics as parenting, sex education, menstruation, childbirth and personal hygiene through case studies and filmed sequences of people and families.

Insects (Ransom) – Mac/PC CD-ROM
Multimedia treatment for minibeasts: contains photo stills, video, spoken commentary and insect sounds.

Life Cycles – Living Library (LDA Multimedia) – Mac/PC CD-ROM
A multimedia CD which relates the lives of amphibians, mammals, insects and birds. A very good reference title – easy to use.

Seashore Life (Anglia Multimedia) – Acorn/Mac/PC CD-ROM
If you are planning a seashore nature trek this is a very handy title for work before or afterwards. You visit typical UK habitats such as sandy shore, rocky shore and estuary, in which you find pictures of animals and plants on which information is given.

Skeleton (Soft Teach Educational) – Acorn/PC
In this lovely little program you can print a life-size skeleton of yourself to assemble. You measure your bones and the computer prints them out full size or, if you prefer, as a scaled-down version.

▶ KS 2–3/P4–S2

Bodywise (Sherston Software) – Acorn
Explore either body parts or body systems, with reading captions and information included with the 3D diagrams and animations. Pupils particularly like the way you can zoom in and out of systems. Everything can be used in pupils' own work and the teacher can configure any or all of it.

Encyclopedia of Animals and Nature (Comptons) – Acorn/Mac/PC CD-ROM
A rather dated, although very useful, reference title with photos and video clips on 1000 creatures.

Eyewitness Virtual Reality: Bird (Dorling Kindersley) – PC CD-ROM
In keeping with most DK CDs, this one is a stunning attention-grabber. The CD puts you in a museum and explores three galleries – anatomy, behaviour and the bird families. Needs lots of time to gain from it.

Trees of Britain (Main Communications) – Acorn/PC
All about classification and facts about trees. Its botanical key is very useful in identifying various species.

▼ Materials and their properties

▶ KS 2–3/P4–S2

States of Matter (New Media Press) – Mac/PC CD-ROM

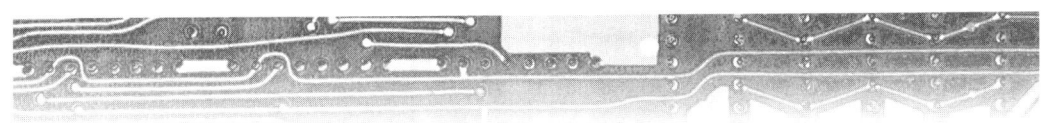

This CD simulates molecule movement under conditions like freezing, condensing and sublimation, filling the niche left when *Moving Molecules* (CMS) was discontinued. This is an excellent resource, perhaps a little too prescriptive at times, but overall an absolute must for anyone studying molecular theory.

▼ Physical processes

► KS 1/P1–3

Smudge the Scientist (Storm Educational Software) – Acorn/PC
The central character, a spaniel, does simple experiments based on floating, growing plants, decay, seasons, and magnets – all relevant to the science curriculum at this level. Overall, this software is likeable and friendly.

► KS 2/P4–7

Atlas of the Solar System (Dorling Kindersley) – PC CD-ROM
Take a flight over the terrain of neigbouring planets. An amazing collection of facts about and references to our solar system.

Being a Scientist (Anglia Multimedia) – Acorn/Mac/PC CD-ROM
An investigation set in a woodland, where pupils try to find out why the trees are vanishing. In order to gain information pupils must interview inhabitants and undertake a series of experiments which involve skills like observation and prediction. As they complete each section they 'construct' a newspaper report.

Encyclopedia of Space and the Universe (Dorling Kindersley) – PC CD-ROM
Over 1,500 subjects organised thematically to complement the curriculum.

A Field Trip to the Sky (Sunburst) – Mac/PC CD-ROM
This has to be the best software to date to teach about the 'Earth and Beyond' section of the National Curriculum. Packed full of investigations, information and images, *A Field Trip to the Sky* is an essential resource.

► KS 2–3/P4–S2

Edison (Designsoft) – PC
This circuit designer is easy to use. Bulbs, buzzers and batteries are all wired up using the mouse. However, this title is particularly good when it comes to teaching and learning principles. There are two versions, DC and AC/DC; both are ideal for extending practical work.

The New Way Things Work (Dorling Kindersley) – Mac/PC CD-ROM
This delightful multimedia CD is really more concerned with technology than science. However, it puts science in the context of inventions such as the battery, the electric motor and the photocopier. One section actually covers scientific principles. Overall, a good reference title with relevant content and stimulating presentation.

▼ General science and reference

Science, as practised in schools, is all about learning by 'doing' and, therefore, to recommend computer-based encyclopedias seems anachronistic. For project work at the computer, however, the CD encyclopedia has several advantages over its traditional printed predecessor:

➡ 27

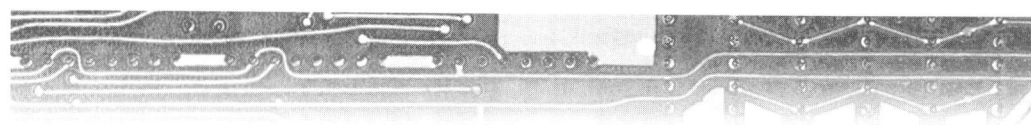

- it is easier to search and sort the information;
- it need not necessarily be based in the library;
- the information you find can be copied and pasted for ease of reference.

Pupils also seem very comfortable with the CD encyclopedia and it becomes something to use and somewhere you can send pupils for answers. The fact that a CD encyclopedia offers multimedia adds to its value, although limited multimedia fits on this type of disk.

On the down side, many CD encyclopedias have been criticised for their non-UK content, although publishers are slowly releasing UK editions.

An interesting feature is that many of the encyclopedias have an Internet button that lets you log onto their website and update with the latest information. The website can offer more detail on a topic or bring information up to date, or even let the user ask an 'expert' a question. Many encyclopedias feature links to information and places on the Internet in order to source additional help.
Some hints and tips on using reference material

- The need for initial work in developing information-handling skills cannot be over-stressed: learning how to use search tools, copy and paste pictures etc.
- Classroom and/or library computers must be ready for use. Train a couple of keen youngsters to switch them on.
- Younger pupils can often look things up without support when the encyclopedia can 'speak' the text.
- Pupils should be focused when they use a CD encyclopedia – an activity sheet is preferable to unsupervised browsing. Other approaches could involve making comparisons, finding evidence for things etc.

- Given half a chance, pupils will simply copy huge amounts of others' text. This must be seen as totally unacceptable; pupils must originate their own text or reference any text they use.
- Similarly, pictures clipped out for pupils' own work should be appropriately captioned to acknowledge sources and indicate reasons for inclusion.
- Pupils should be encouraged to present a short list of their sources of information.

▼ Encyclopedias

► KS 1–2/P1–7

Kingfisher Micropedia (ESM Software) – Acorn CD-ROM
Based on the popular Kingfisher Children's Encyclopedia, the CD version has excellent cross-referencing, a spoken index and a built-in notepad. There are 1300 spoken entries with 1600 pictures under 12 topics.

Sammy's Science House (Inclusive Technology) – Mac/PC CD-ROM
This program comprises five activities where pupils can practise sequencing, classifying, and looking at cause and effect. It covers living things, machines, seasons and weather. A good title for younger pupils.

► KS 2/P4–7

Encyclopedia of Science 2.0 (Dorling Kindersley) – PC CD-ROM
This CD shows you how science works using many full-colour photographs, diagrams, charts, cutaway artworks and detailed illustrations. It is thematically organised and packed with facts, figures and statistics.

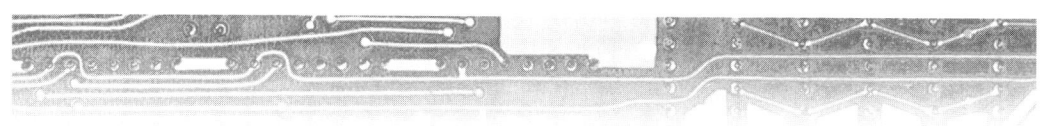

◎ *The Oxford Children's Encyclopedia* (OUP) – PC CD-ROM
An excellent source for the age group; very popular in schools.

◎ *Science Explorer* (Granada Learning) – Acorn/Mac/PC CD-ROM
Based on an interactive science museum where you visit galleries and explore things, this excellent CD has that rare commodity, flair. It covers lots of science at just the right level. There is a good balance of topics: animals, space, forces, materials and electricity, and things to find out. There are experiments to do and a quiz to check knowledge.

▶ KS 2–3/P4–S2

◎ *Eyewitness Children's Encyclopedia* (Dorling Kindersley) – PC CD-ROM
This CD has the customary stunning effects.

◎ *Grolier Encyclopedia Deluxe 2000* (Grolier) – Mac/PC CD-ROM
The computer version of the very well-known book title.

◎ *World Book Multimedia Encyclopedia 2000* (World Book) – Mac/PC CD-ROM
Currently one of the best encyclopedias around; has a very good search system and a related website which provides comprehensive National Curriculum links as well as updates.

◎ *PictureBase* (AVP) – Acorn/PC CD-ROM
PictureBase presents learning sequences and resources in subject modules. A module consists of a series of images each with its own descriptive text, video and sound files which are grouped in National Curriculum themes. The title *PictureBase* is a bit misleading, for it is a database capable of limitless expansion and of controlling all forms of media – text, high-quality pictures, sound and video. Where it differs from its contemporaries is that it can access the data on any number of CDs and, in addition, permits teachers to tailor the material extensively for their own purposes.

Some of the titles available in the *Picture Base* series are: *Habitats of the British Isles*; *World Habitats*; *Life and Living Processes*; *Earth and Atmosphere*; *Materials*; *Rocks, Minerals and Fossils*; and *Physical Processes*.

It is worth noting that AVP have made all their titles available via AVPnet which offers an intranet version of all the above and more. As the content is totally related to the National Curriculum and all text, pictures, photos etc. are freely available, this provides a wonderful opportunity to develop an intranet of resources.

Science links in the DfEE QCA ICT Scheme of Work ▼

Unit	Activity	Link with science
1A	An introduction to modelling	sequencing pictures and text
1B	Using a word bank	reports, descriptions, lists etc.
1C	The information around us	data handling
1D	Labelling and classifying	sorting objects
1E	Representing information graphically: pictograms	classifying objects, undertaking investigations
1F	Understanding instructions and making things happen	pushes and pulls
2A	Writing stories: communicating information using text	reports, descriptions, lists etc.
2B	Creating pictures	diagrams, illustrations of work
2C	Finding information	CD-ROM, WWW references to science topic
2D	Routes: controlling a floor turtle	application of forces – pushes and pulls
2E	Questions and answers	variation
3A	Combining text and graphics	reports, descriptions, lists etc.
3B	Manipulating sound	application of science work in music
3C	Introduction to databases	data handling and presentation
3D	Exploring simulations	application of concepts and knowledge gained
3E	E-mail	gathering data, developing collaborative projects
4A	Writing for different audiences	reports, descriptions, lists etc.
4B	Developing images using repeating patterns	diagrams, copying patterns in nature
4C	Branching databases	classifying plants and animals, objects
4D	Collecting and presenting information: questionnaires and charts	presenting graphs and charts
4E	Modelling effects on screen	friction
5A	Graphical modelling	drawing diagrams
5B	Analysing data and asking questions: using complex searches	investigating possible relationships between data
5C	Evaluating information, checking accuracy and questioning plausibility	all data-handling activities
5D	Introduction to spreadsheets	exploring scientific models
5E	Controlling devices	application of forces – pushes and pulls
5F	Monitoring environmental conditions and changes	changing state
6A	Multimedia presentation	reports, descriptions, presenting information
6B	Spreadsheet modelling	exploring scientific models
6C	Control and monitoring – What happens when …?	application of forces – pushes and pulls, cause and effect
6D	Using the Internet to search large databases and to interpret information	how we see things

For further details on how each activity relates to the DfEE QCA Schemes of Work for science and ICT, please refer to our website at www.nelsonthornes.com/icthandbooks.

5–14 National Guidelines for Scotland ▼

The creation of separate and distinct guidelines for 5–14 Information and Communications Technology reflects many changes in society, and, therefore, in education. The increasing emphasis on the use of computer technology for word processing, databases and spreadsheets, the power of the Internet and the acquisitions of the skills required to access this powerful tool, have necessitated a change in curricula throughout Europe

The ICT handbooks website includes correlation charts linking the *Environmental Studies – Science: 5–14 National Guidelines* and the related *ICT: 5–14 National Guidelines*. These charts further highlight the three strands for developing skills in science and identify activities from the handbook that support each of them. These strands include:

- preparing for tasks
- carrying out tasks
- reviewing and reporting on tasks.

For ICT, a similar chart is provided, identifying handbook avtivities that support the seven ICT strands such as 'Creating and presenting' and 'Collecting and analysing'.

It is also important to note that the activities also support the progression across all of these strands moving the pupils away from being supported to becoming independent users of ICT.

Finally, the revised *5–14 National Guidelines: Environmental Studies* (Learning and Teaching Scotland, 2000) emphasize the importance of ICT as a means of enhancing teaching and learning in environmental studies, as follows:

- Creating and presenting – using ICT so that pupils can create and present their own ideas and other material.

- Collecting and analysing – using ICT tools to collect and analyse information, such as databases and spreadsheets, and to solve problems.

- Searching and researching – using resources such as CD-ROMs and the Internet to allow pupils to search for information and to research topics.

- Controlling and modelling – using computers to instruct and control devices as well as to take measurements of, and model, the environment.

Teachers are able to identify activities that support these strands using the ICT Handbooks website at www.nelsonthornes.com/icthandbooks.

Introducing Control: What Makes It Go? ▼

Learning objectives ▼

Pupils learn to:
- give instructions using the keypad;
- control directional movement;
- begin to appreciate the need for accuracy and definition.

ICT resources ▼

A floor robot such as Roamer (Valiant Technology) or PIP (Swallow Systems) or, better still, a table-top robot such as Pixie (Swallow Systems)

Vocabulary ▼

instructions
order
control
robot

▼ Introduction

- Discuss the sequence of instructions involved in things familiar to the pupils, for example using a tape recorder, video player, toys, traffic lights etc. This should be in the context of 'What makes it go?'
- Encourage pupils to recognise that a floor/table-top robot is not alive but can only follow instructions. Make the robot travel to a marked area and then follow a simple course to a target, using commands such as Forward, Back, Left, Right etc. Demonstrate how to clear the memory before providing new instructions.
- Practise getting the robot to a particular spot using the fewest possible instructions. Encourage pupils to make predictions of how many will be needed.

▼ Suggested activities

- Pupils 'control' each other in pairs. One gives a command which their partner must follow. Try this activity outside or in the hall.
- Pupils make the robot travel between two points, or try to make it arrive on a card square placed on the table or floor (this could have a relevant picture on it).
- Encourage pupils to talk about what they do with the whole class.

▼ Assessment focus

Pupils:
- know that machines and devices have to be controlled;
- know that some machines work by using the correct sequence of actions;
- learn that the sequence of instructions must be correct to achieve the desired results;
- recognise that instructions can be given in a 'natural' language.

 YEAR R / P1

Using a Word Bank ▼

Learning objectives ▼

Pupils learn to:
- recognise letters from their name on the keyboard;
- type their own names accurately;
- use a mouse with a degree of hand-eye co-ordination;
- select using the correct button on the mouse.

ICT resources ▼

Clicker 4 (Crick Software) plus a word processor

Vocabulary ▼

type
delete
add
word bank

▼ Introduction

- Prepare a simple sentence with a child's name missing, for example '. . . likes apples.'
- Demonstrate how to use the keyboard to type a name, emphasising not keeping the finger on a key but 'tapping' it.
- Prepare an appropriate word bank with the pupils' names, using *Clicker*.
- Show the class how to select their name from the word bank using the mouse.
- Demonstrate how to hear the word spoken if they are unsure from its visual clues.

▼ Suggested activities

- Each pupil proceeds by clicking in the right part of the sentence and typing the letters of their own name.
- The less able can enter their names from the *Clicker* word bank to complete the sentence.
- When complete, print each pupil a copy and they can draw themselves to illustrate it.

▼ Assessment focus

This work can be adapted to any unit for Year R / P1. The difficulty of the ICT involved can be adapted as pupils' language skills increase.

- Pupils become familiar with the keyboard.
- Pupils learn that text can be entered from a prepared word bank.

YEAR R / P1

33

Sequencing: Information Around Us ▼

Learning objectives ▼

Pupils learn that:
- information can be presented in a variety of forms;
- computers use text, pictures, animations and sounds to convey information.

ICT resources ▼

Sequences (Granada Learning)

Vocabulary ▼

information
button/icon
CD-ROM
text
graphics

▼ Introduction

- Being able to sequence correctly is an essential basic skill. *Sequences* is an excellent vehicle for learning to handle CD-based information.
- Discuss care and safety in handling CDs, and loading and running the software.
- Discuss how tasks are found by using the simple menus system. Demonstrate how to choose tasks by using menus and icons.
- Show pupils how to retrace their steps using the on screen buttons.

▼ Suggested activities

- Ask the children to explore the tasks on the Sequences CD-ROM.
- Question them on how the program uses text, pictures, icons, animations and sounds to show what is happening. For example, ask them 'How do you know where to click?' and 'What is used to tell you a correct answer?'

▼ Assessment focus

Pupils recognise:
- that computer programs use sounds, text and pictures to convey information.
- some of the conventions used in computer programs to represent information.

YEAR R / P1

Us, Our Senses – Assembling Text and Pictures ▼

Learning objectives ▼

Pupils learn to:
- use ICT to organise words and pictures;
- use the mouse to make selections and organise elements using drag and drop techniques;
- apply what they learn when matching pictures to labels in science.

ICT resources ▼

My World 2 and the Key Stage file 'Biology', or *My World 3* and *My World of Science* (all SEMERC)

Vocabulary ▼

drag
drop

▼ Introduction

Demonstrate to the class how to:

- use *My World* with the 'Biology' file loaded. Encourage the more able pupils to load and run the software independently;
- choose, move and place objects so that they fit into a predetermined space, and then how to remove or reject them;
- add a simple one-word caption;
- print out the final picture.

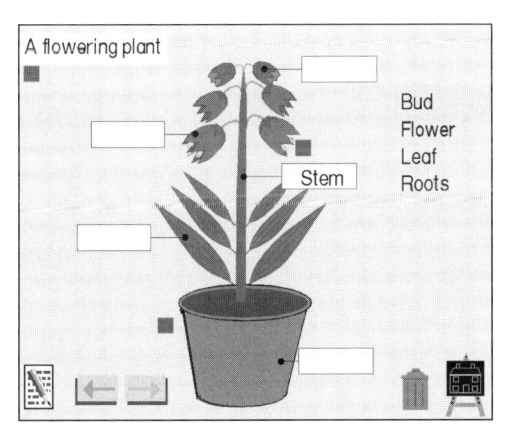

▼ Suggested activities

- Pupils proceed with the software in pairs. Each pair creates a 'screen' containing pictures with simple captions.

▼ Assessment focus

Pupils:

- control the mouse effectively;
- drag the appropriate words into the correct positions;
- assemble pictures with appropriate text.

YEAR R / P1

Assembling Text and Pictures ▼

Learning objectives ▼

Pupils learn to:
- recognise letters on the keyboard and screen;
- type words accurately;
- select using the correct button on the mouse.

ICT resources ▼

My World 2 and 'Me' file, or *My World 3* and *My World of Science* (all SEMERC)

Vocabulary ▼

mouse
pointer
left/right button
click select
drag
screen/display

▼ Introduction

- Discuss with the pupils their earlier experiences of using a computer at home or elsewhere. Ask them to describe what computers are used for.
- Set up the *My World* software.
- Demonstrate how to:
  - load the screen 'Me';
  - drag and drop the various items to complete each simple sentence/picture (the software is self-explanatory);
  - print out when all is complete.

My name is Mia

I am a girl

cat
dog

I am not a boy

I am not a

▼ Suggested activities

- Each pupil proceeds through the software at their own pace. Working in pairs often helps to eliminate errors, as one pupil can act as a 'checker'.

▼ Assessment focus

Pupils:
- recognise simple words and pictures on screen;
- begin to learn that computers have a variety of uses;
- learn that ICT can be used to assemble text and pictures.

YEAR 1 / P2

Using a Simulation ▼

Learning objectives ▼

Pupils learn:
- that, using ICT, a process can be modelled so that results can be seen more quickly;
- to manipulate simple variables;
- to make decisions based on their learning and see the consequences.

ICT resources ▼

Smudge the Scientist (Storm Educational Software): Disk 1: 'Plants and plant growth'

Vocabulary ▼

modelling
load
run
print

▼ Introduction

This software is not the best around and could do with some redesign but it does contain a simple simulation suitable for this year group. The simulation concerns the successful germination and growth of a bed of sunflowers. The variables are weather items: sun, rain and snow, and a watering can.

- Demonstrate to class how to load and run the software. Encourage the more able pupils to load and run the software independently.
- Explain that the task is to make the sunflowers grow in the shortest possible time without killing them in the process.
- Show the magnifying glass icon, which presents information, and encourage use of the note pad if needed.
- Show how to print the screen.

▼ Suggested activities

- Pupils proceed with the software in pairs. After each turn the screen should be printed out and brought to the teacher as proof of success.
- Discuss their choice of variables and how they led to success or failure.
- The software has a useful 'naming parts' section which could be used to assess whether the pupils can successfully name the parts of a plant. It is similar to a *My World* screen.

▼ Assessment focus

Pupils:
- choose variables in a considered fashion;
- realise that the simulation does not cover all the variables affecting plant growth (what does it miss?)
- print out the final screen as evidence.

YEAR 1 / P2

Using a Word Bank

Learning objectives

Pupils learn:
- that text can be entered from a prepared word bank;
- to use a word bank to create a simple sentence.

ICT resources

Clicker 4 (Crick Software) plus a word processor

Vocabulary

select
delete

▼ Introduction

- Prepare:
  - a list of simple sentences with phrases missing;
  - an appropriate word bank (using *Clicker*) related to the materials you are studying.
- Demonstrate how to:
  - select words from the word bank using the mouse;
  - hear the phrase spoken if they are unsure from its visual clues.
- Explain that the pupils are going to produce sentences about materials. They select the initial sentence and add their choice of phrases from the *Clicker* word bank.

▼ Suggested activities

- In pairs, pupils select incomplete sentences and add a phrase from the *Clicker* word bank to complete them.
- Encourage the more able pupils to add more information of their own to each sentence.
- When complete, each pupil should print themselves a copy and illustrate it.

▼ Assessment focus

Pupils:
- communicate ideas by selecting and adding text;
- create a complete and accurate sentence.

Editing a Picture ▼

Learning objectives ▼

Pupils learn to:
- recognise icons representing tools;
- make colour choices from a palette;
- use a mouse with a degree of hand-eye co-ordination;
- select using the correct button on the mouse.

ICT resources ▼

Dazzle Plus (SEMERC) or an alternative first-paint program. Ideally, a device such as the Easy Painter Tablet (SEMERC) will help pupils to draw/select with greater accuracy.

Vocabulary ▼

load
save
fill
brush
undo
palette

▼ Introduction

- Configure the painting program to its simplest level (in *Dazzle Plus* called 'Simple').
- Demonstrate how to:
  - load and run the program;
  - load a line drawing file from the Picture icon;
  - use the icons available (brush, fill, save and print);
  - use the Fill tool by choosing a colour from the palette and clicking over the area to be filled;
  - 'undo' a mistake by refilling in the desired colour. When all else fails, demonstrate how to load another line drawing template in order to begin again.

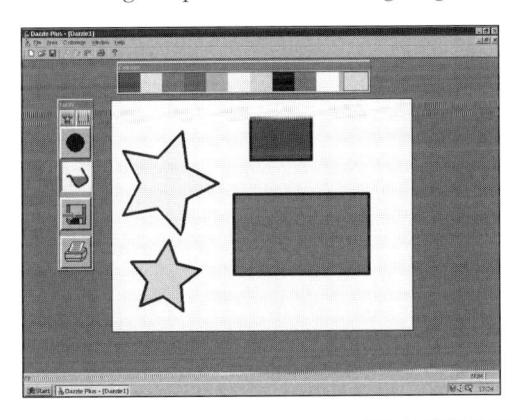

▼ Suggested activities

- Each pupil chooses a line drawing template from those provided and 'colours' it in.
- When complete, the work should be saved and a copy printed out.

▼ Assessment focus

Pupils become:
- aware that ICT can be used to paint and draw;
- familiar with the mouse, icon and keyboard.

YEAR 1 / P2

Control: Understanding Instructions and Making Things Happen ▼

Learning objectives ▼

Pupils learn to:
- sequence: giving and interpreting instructions;
- use a control language based on directional movement;
- appreciate the need for accuracy and definition.

ICT resources ▼

A floor robot such as Roamer (Valiant Technology) or PIP (Swallow Systems)

Vocabulary ▼

sequence
instructions
order
control

▼ Introduction

- Discuss the sequence of instructions involved in things familiar to the pupils, for example using a tape recorder, video player, toys, traffic lights etc.
- Encourage pupils to recognise that a floor robot is not alive but can only follow instructions. Make the robot travel to a marked area and then follow a simple course to a target, using commands such as Forward, Back, Left, Right etc. Demonstrate how to clear the memory before providing new instructions.
- Practise getting the robot to a particular spot using the fewest possible instructions. Encourage pupils to make predictions of how many will be needed.

▼ Suggested activities

Pupils:
- 'control' each other in pairs. One gives a command which their partner must follow. Try this activity outside or in the hall;
- make the robot travel between two points, or try to knock down a tower of play bricks;
- record their instructions.

▼ Assessment focus

Pupils:
- know that machines and devices have to be controlled;
- know that some machines work by using the correct sequence of actions;
- learn that the sequence of instructions must be correct to achieve the desired results;
- recognise that instructions can be given in a 'natural' language.

YEAR 1 / P2

Creating Sounds ▼

Learning objectives ▼

Pupils learn to:
- use a music program to create a composition;
- use the most appropriate tools for their purpose;
- develop a composition and modify ICT accordingly.

ICT resources ▼

A music program such as *Compose World* (SEMERC), *Music Games* (Inclusive Technology)

Vocabulary ▼

compose
icons
sounds library
high/low notes
phrase

▼ Introduction

Demonstrate how to:
- load and run the software;
- assemble icons to produce tunes.

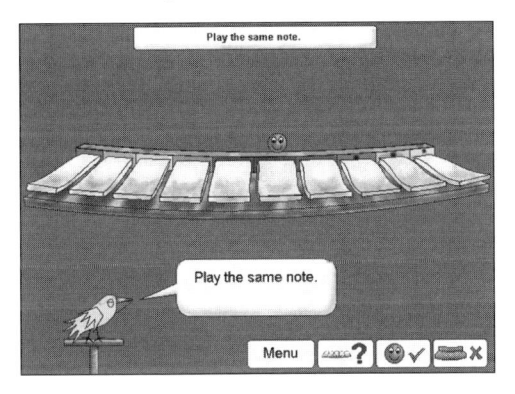

▼ Suggested activities

- Individually, pupils create a composition, which could be a tune or a 'sound picture'. This should be saved.
- When enough compositions have been saved, the pupils could listen to each one in turn; encourage them to make constructive comments. Groups could be encouraged to extend or add new 'movements' to another group's composition.

▼ Assessment focus

Pupils learn:
- that ICT can be used to create and edit music;
- that they can modify sounds and undo mistakes;
- to save their work regularly as they go along.

Assembling Text and Pictures ▼

Learning objectives ▼

Pupils learn to:
- recognise letters on the keyboard and screen;
- type words accurately;
- use a mouse with a degree of hand-eye coordination;
- select using the correct button on the mouse.

ICT resources ▼

My World 2 and 'Basic Screens' file, or *My World 3* and *My World of Science* (all SEMERC)

Vocabulary ▼

mouse
pointer
left/right button
click select
drag
screen/display

▼ Introduction

- Decide on the content of the *My World* file you want the pupils to use, taking into account their level of ICT skill.
- Use the 'Basic Screens' section to find the 'Body' and 'Face' screens.
- Show pupils how to load and run the *My World* software and how to load the 'Body' and 'Face' screens.
- Remind pupils how to:
  - drag and drop the the body part name and an arrow to complete the caption (the software is self-explanatory);
  - print out when all is complete.

▼ Suggested activities

Each pupil proceeds at their own pace. Working in pairs often helps to eliminate errors, as one pupil can act as a 'checker'.

▼ Assessment focus

- The teacher should recognise that a *My World* activity provides pupils with the opportunity to demonstrate the following ICT skills: load software; load files; manipulate images and text; and print and save work.
- Pupils
  - recognise simple words and pictures on screen;
  - begin to learn that computers have a variety of uses;
  - learn that ICT can be used to assemble text and pictures.

YEAR 2 / P3

Finding Information: CD-ROM ▼

Learning objectives ▼

Pupils learn to:
- navigate a CD-ROM;
- search a CD-ROM;
- choose the most appropriate search technique for their purpose;
- use an 'expert' (key system) to identify unknown garden creatures.

ICT resources ▼

Garden Wildlife (Anglia Multimedia)

Vocabulary ▼

search
CD-ROM
menu
index
keyword
links

▼ Introduction

- Using the *Garden Wildlife* CD, discuss care and safety in handling CDs, loading and running the software.
- Discuss how information is found in reference books using an index system.
- Demonstrate
  - how to locate information using menus and icons;
  - how text can be found using *Garden Wildlife*'s 'find text' searching mechanism;
  - how pupils can retrace their steps using the on-screen buttons.

▼ Suggested activities

- Using the techniques introduced above, set pupils the task of looking at two contrasting environments (for example the garden and the park) and of locating and gathering information. This can be printed out directly, or notes may be made in the software's 'note pad', which can be printed on completion.
- Alternatively, set pupils the task of searching for all occurrences of a particular species.
- An additional activity could be using the 'expert' to help pupils identify creatures found during a field trip.

This CD is so comprehensive it allows a great deal of flexibility in how you integrate it with the 'local plants and animals' topic.

▼ Assessment focus

Demonstrate how to:
- recognise that CDs store large amounts of information;
- use simple search tools;
- use menus to locate information;
- begin to use keywords to search for information.

YEAR 2 / P3

Representing Information Graphically

Learning objectives

Pupils learn:
- to create pictograms to represent information graphically;
- that data represented graphically can be easier to understand;
- to use pictograms to answer simple questions.

ICT resources

Pictogram software such as *Pictogram 2* (Kudlian Soft)

Vocabulary

pictogram

▼ Introduction

- Show pupils how pictures can be used to represent data and to build up a pictogram graph.
- Ask pupils to draw pictures of different minibeasts. These pictures could be sorted into sets and arranged on the wall to make a class pictogram. Ask the pupils questions such as: 'What seems to be the most common creature with wings?', 'The least common?' etc.
- Show the class how to use *Pictogram 2* by using the file 'minibeasts' provided. Build up the pictogram to match the one on the wall display. Make comparisons between paper and computer versions. Print out the computer version and add it to the display.
- Before showing pupils the software, decide which files you wish to use. Among *Pictogram 2*'s files are: fruits, vegetables, minibeasts, pets, eye colour. Ensure that the pupils have a set of related images, objects etc to assemble and count.

▼ Suggested activities

Pupils:
- (in pairs) create a pictogram using the software;
- answer several simple questions based on the pictogram;
- save their work when complete and print out a copy.

▼ Assessment focus

- Data which has been collected can be represented as pictograms.
- ICT can be used to create pictograms.

YEAR 2 / P3

Collecting, Assembling and Interrogating Information: a Database ▼

Learning objectives ▼

Pupils will:
- collect, process and display data;
- begin to understand how to use databases to handle data.

ICT resources ▼

A database program such as *DataSweet* (Kudlian Soft) or *Granada Database* (Granada Learning)

Vocabulary ▼

database
heading
file
record
search

▼ Introduction

- Have a range of materials available which will conform to the headings you have chosen.
- Construct a simple database, with each entry having about five or six fields: 'colour', 'weight', 'texture' etc.
- Prepare a small questionnaire giving clues and suggestions on how to search.
- Introduce the database software as a class lesson using one of the sample files.
- Remind pupils that a database is a collection of records, and each record has headings and information.
- Show them
  - the template file you have created and discuss the headings;
  - how to load, enter and save data;
  - how to perform simple searches for information.

▼ Suggested activities

Pupils:
- examine (in pairs) one of the materials, entering their findings in the database (this will need checking for spelling etc at the end of each day);
- answer their questionnaire using the completed database to search for the information.

▼ Assessment focus

Pupils use database software to record and query data.

YEAR 2 / P3

Controlling a Floor Robot ▼

Learning objectives ▼

Pupils learn to:
- produce an accurate set of instructions;
- accurately predict the result of a set of instructions;
- recognise that control devices follow instructions.

ICT resources ▼

A floor robot such as Roamer (Valiant Technology) or Pixie/PIP (Swallow Systems)

Vocabulary ▼

control devices
instructions
data
commands
program

▼ Introduction

- Encourage pupils to recognise that a floor robot is not alive but can only follow instructions. Make the robot travel to a marked area and then follow a simple course to a target, using commands such as Forward, Back, Left, Right etc.
- Demonstrate how to:
  - clear the memory before providing new instructions;
  - enter a sequence of instructions to make the robot perform forward movement, turn, forward movement.

▼ Suggested activities

- Make a simple maze of 'streets' from paper or card. Along the 'streets' place names of pupils in the class (or pictures of houses, places to visit etc.).
- In pairs, pupils program the robot to visit two or more 'places' in a predetermined sequence. They should be encouraged to record their sequence of instructions.

▼ Assessment focus

- Control devices:
  - must be programmed;
  - follow instructions that can contain numerical data.
- Instructions can be sequenced for more complicated tasks.

YEAR 2 / P3

Assembling Text and Pictures ▼

Learning objectives ▼

Pupils learn to:
- use ICT as a means of organising words and pictures;
- use the mouse to organise elements using drag and drop techniques;
- apply what they learn when matching pictures to labels in science.

ICT resources ▼

My World 2 and the Key Stage 1 file 'Physical Processes', or *My World 3* and *My World of Science* (all SEMERC)

Vocabulary ▼

pointer
select
menu
options
screen

▼ Introduction

Remind pupils how to:

- use *My World* with the 'Biology' file loaded. Encourage the more able pupils to load and run the software independently, including loading the 'Physical Processes' screen;
- choose, move and place objects so that they fit into predetermined spaces, and then how to remove or reject them;
- type text and place and reject it;
- save their completed work and print it out. Demonstrate some of the options for printing that *My World* offers, emphasising the advantages of each. For example, print with no background so that the completed image can be cut out and pasted into other work.

▼ Suggested activities

Pupils proceed in pairs, each creating a 'screen' containing pictures with simple captions. This activity can take place throughout Unit 3's half term in England, as there are screens suited to work throughout the topic.

▼ Assessment focus

Pupils:

- drag the appropriate words and images into the correct positions;
- assemble pictures with appropriate text.

YEAR 2 / P3

Combining Text and Graphics Using a Website

Learning objectives

Pupils learn to:
- access current data from the Internet
- copy and paste images from the website into a word processor and add own text

ICT resources

Internet connected computer(s), printer(s) and Microsoft® Word
Websites:
www.healthyteeth.org/teeth.html#2 (Nova Scotia Dental Association);
www.bbc.co.uk/health/teeth/index.shtml (BBC Online Teeth Website);
http://dgl.microsoft.com/ (Microsoft's Design Gallery Online)

Vocabulary

website
URL
logging on
copy-and-paste

Introduction

This activity combines the use of a website to gain information and the ability to copy and paste images with word processing. It is important that the teacher visits the site and reads the information available about the development of teeth in humans. Try to adapt the pupil's task according to ability and focus. Pupils will probably need a demonstration of how to proceed in logging on to the Internet and to locate the URLs. If this is perceived as being too difficult then an adult could log on prior to the lesson and bookmark the sites in order that the pupils can access them more easily.

Suggested activities

Pupils:
- locate the Healthy Teeth and BBC Teeth websites and read the information about teeth, making notes as they go.
- open the word processor and write up in their own words information they have discovered.
- log onto the Microsoft Design Gallery and fill in the fields as follows: search for 'teeth'; search in 'everywhere'; results in 'clip art'; and order by 'colourful'.
- can download a relevant clip to add to their own information. They may need help in learning how to right-click and 'copy' on the graphic in the Design Window and right-click and 'paste' on their work screen.

Assessment focus

- Is the information relevant to what the pupils have to find out?
- Why should you not copy and edit the information?

YEAR 3 / P4

Creating a Simple Spreadsheet ▼

Learning objectives ▼

Pupils learn that:
- a spreadsheet can be used to record and analyse information;
- information can be graphically displayed using a spreadsheet.

ICT resources ▼

A simple spreadsheet program such as *Granada Spreadsheet* (Granada Learning)

Vocabulary ▼

spreadsheet
cell
enter
delete
save
scatter graph

▼ Introduction

- Introduce:
  - a spreadsheet program by demonstrating using one of the ready-made files accompanying the software. Emphasise that a spreadsheet is a program which is very good for making graphs of collected data;
  - the prepared template file containing column headings.
- Show pupils how data can be entered into each of the cells and deleted if a mistake is made.

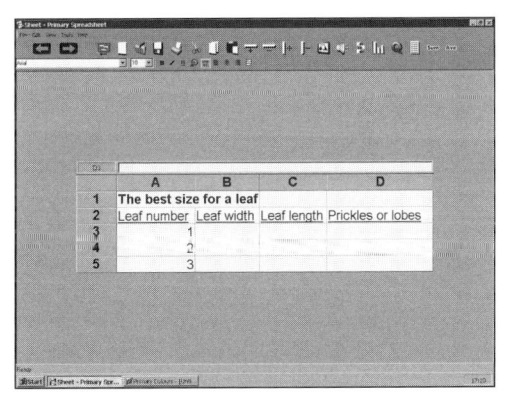

▼ Suggested activities

- Typically, leaves from any one tree can range in size
- The pupils each gather one leaf from a single tree and measure its length, breadth and the number of lobes or prickles it has. A mixed sample of about 30 leaves should do.
- Each pupil enters the measurements into the prepared spreadsheet, which can be used to print a graph to analyse their findings.
- More able pupils can look for patterns in the data and draw a scatter graph to show this.

▼ Assessment focus

- Is there a typical size for a leaf?
- Do larger leaves have more lobes or prickles?

YEAR 3 / P4

Monitoring Temperature ▼

Learning objectives ▼

Pupils learn to:
- take temperature measurements automatically;
- interpret a line graph;
- use sensors correctly.

ICT resources ▼

EcoLog and *Sensing Science Primary* software (both Data Harvest) or equivalent monitoring system

Vocabulary ▼

sensor
data-logger
connection
data recording

▼ Introduction

- Using a thermometer and temperature sensor, discuss with the pupils similarities and differences, pointing out the advantage of using ICT equipment for measuring (accuracy, remote capability etc).
- Discuss how sensors work by demonstrating using a temperature sensor and *Sensing Science Primary* software.
- As a whole-class lesson, demonstrate the software with a sensor connected to establish familiarity.

▼ Suggested activities

- Tell pupils that their task is to discover which material would make the best gloves for winter-time. Discuss how to go about the task, including the safety issues.
- In small groups, tell pupils to wrap different materials around pairs of cups/drinks cans filled with warm water.
- Get pupils to use two temperature sensors to monitor the temperature of each pair of cups using *Sensing Science Graph Plus*.

▼ Assessment focus

- What types of material should work best?
- Is one material as good as any other?
- Which material insulates best?
- Which one is the poorest insulator?

YEAR 3 / P4

Creating a Key System using a Branching Database ▼

Learning objectives ▼

Pupils learn that:
- a branching tree diagram can be used to organise information;
- yes/no questions can divide a set of objects into subsets and that a sequence of such questions can uniquely identify an object;
- a branching database can be searched in order to identify an object.

ICT resources ▼

Granada Branch (Granada Learning) or similar branching database software

Vocabulary ▼

branching database
key system

▼ Introduction

- Introduce a branching database by demonstrating with one of the ready-made files that come with the software.
- Make a set of cards each with a picture of a different rock and a few key features on the back. These could be a crystalline structure and a colour. Pupils sort these into sets, recording their criteria. Use strips of card/paper to link the sets together.

▼ Suggested activities

- The database can be started by linking two rocks, each from the two different sets, and then thinking of a question to distinguish one rock from the other. By picking one card at a time, the pupils can work through the program adding each rock as the database grows.
- Pupils can try out the key to check for errors and to see if it 'works'. The finished database can be used as an example of a key system and can be added to at any time.

▼ Assessment focus

- Pupils will need to be familiar with dividing sets of objects into subsets.
- Phrasing the 'right' question is very important and may need some discussion: 'Is it rigid?' is more useful than 'Is it hard?'
- A branching database makes a useful key for identification.

YEAR 3 / P4

Collecting, Assembling and Interrogating Information: a Database ▼

Learning objectives ▼

Pupils learn to:
- collect, process and display data;
- understand how to use databases to handle data.

ICT resources ▼

A database program such as *Junior Pinpoint* (Logotron) or *Granada Database* (Granada Learning)

Vocabulary ▼

database
heading
file
record
search

▼ Introduction

- Have a range of materials available that will conform to the headings you have chosen.
- Construct a simple database with each entry having about six to eight fields: 'colour', 'weight', 'texture', 'attracted to magnet', 'springy', 'soft or hard', 'float or sink' etc. If your software permits it, try to use restricted fields when setting up a database. Using this system, the pupils enter their observations by selecting their answer to a question from a multiple-choice selection. This not only ensures uniformity of input but is also a much quicker method of entering material.
- Prepare a small questionnaire giving clues and suggestions on how to search.
- Introduce the database software as a class lesson using one of the supplied sample files.
- Remind pupils that a database is a collection of records, each of which has headings and information.
- Show them your prepared template file and discuss the headings.
- Demonstrate how to:
    - load, enter and save data;
    - perform simple searches for information.

▼ Suggested activities

- In pairs, pupils examine one of the materials, entering their findings in one of the records of the database (this will need checking for spelling at the end of each day).
- Pupils answer their questionnaire using the completed database to search for the information.

▼ Assessment focus

Pupils use database software to record and query data.

YEAR 3 / P4

Investigating the Light Sensor ▼

Learning objectives ▼

Pupils learn that:
- a light sensor responds quickly to change in light;
- the sensor gives a reading;
- light levels can be measured.

ICT resources ▼

EcoLog and *Sensing Science Primary* software (both Data Harvest) or equivalent monitoring system
Learning resources: electric torch, light from a window, candle, desk lamp, a variety of fabrics

Vocabulary ▼

light sensor
gauge
data-logger

▼ Introduction

- Use the light sensor to introduce the *Sensing Science Primary* screen displays.
- Load the *Sensing Science Primary* software, choosing colour change, Gauge, Bar and Number displays.
- Explain and demonstrate how each display shows in a different way whether there is more or less light.

▼ Suggested activities

- Pupils place the sensor so that it:
  - points to the brightest light and observe the displays;
  - points to the dark and observe the displays.
- Which light source is the best to read by? Pupils:
  - use the sensor to place a range of light sources in order of brightness;
  - cover the light sensor with different materials in turn and place them in order of opacity.

▼ Assessment focus

- What happens to the Change display when the sensor is pointed to the brightest light source?
- What happens to the Bar display when you move the sensors from bright to dark?
- Which display shows the results best?
- How will you make the tests fair?

YEAR 3 / P4

Finding Information from a CD-ROM ▼

Learning objectives ▼

Pupils learn that:
- in order to get the information you want you must search the CD-ROM;
- information stored electronically can be saved for their own use;
- the information is not theirs but the copyright holder's;
- sources of information should be clearly noted.

ICT resources ▼

A CD-ROM encyclopedia

Vocabulary ▼

CD-ROM
searching
editing
cut and paste
font size
image size

▼ Introduction

- Become familiar with the content of the CD (confirm that it does actually contain information about scientists) and how to use the search facility.
- Introduce the CD in a whole-class lesson, demonstrating that the wealth of information can lead to being 'lost'.
- Show how to get a piece of information about an unrelated topic using the search facility.
- Show how to save the information, emphasising that the saved material is for reference only.
- Quit the CD and load DTP software, importing the information. Show the class how to use the software to originate their own text about their research topic.

▼ Suggested activities

The pupils:
- search the CD (in pairs) to find information about famous scientists;
- save information and any illustrations;
- use DTP software to compile their own presentations on the scientist, using their search results for reference;
- use completed presentations as part of a science display in the classroom.

▼ Assessment focus

- Why should you not copy and edit the saved information?
- How do CD-ROMs and printed encyclopedias compare?
- Do you know the meaning of . . . ? What is a more simple way to say . . . ?
- How will you make your presentation attractive?
- Which font(s) suit(s) this piece?
- Where will you place the picture and the text?

YEAR 4 / P 5

Developing a Database of Minibeasts and Their Habitats ▼

Learning objectives ▼

Pupils learn to:
- select those fields which are significant;
- create a data-capture form and print it out;
- research minibeasts using books and other media;
- enter data gathered;
- interpret the data using a database's search and graphing facilities.

ICT resources ▼

A database program such as *Junior Pinpoint* (Logotron) or *Granada Database* (Granada Learning); a CD-ROM such as *Creepy Crawlies* (Cumana) as an information source

Vocabulary ▼

database
field
field name
file
record
search
sort

▼ Introduction

- Introduce the database software as a class lesson, using one of the provided sample files.
- Remind pupils that a database is a collection of records, each consisting of fields or headings and data.
- Show them how to load, edit and save data.

▼ Suggested activities

- Either as a class activity or in small groups, pupils decide which fields (headings) they want to include in their minibeasts database.
- Using the database software, they enter these and create the layout. This should be printed out as a data-capture form.
- Individually, pupils research information books/CDs to find information about minibeasts to enter onto their forms.
- In pairs, pupils enter the data into the database.
- The completed database should be checked and amended if necessary by more able members of the class.
- Pupils then try to find the answers to the key questions below and should be encouraged to look for patterns in the data.

▼ Assessment focus

- Which minibeasts live in the soil? Do they have anything in common?
- Which minibeasts have eight legs?
- Do any spiders have wings?
- Which creatures have two wings?
- Which creatures have four wings/more than four wings?

YEAR 4 / P5

Exploring Temperature: Whose Hands are Warmer?

Learning objectives

Pupils learn that:
- more than one sensor can be used at a time;
- using two temperature sensors allows measurements to be compared;
- rubbing the temperature sensor has an effect.

ICT resources

EcoLog and *Sensing Science Primary* software (both Data Harvest) or equivalent monitoring system; two separate temperature sensors

Vocabulary

temperature sensor

▼ Introduction

- With EcoLog connected to the computer, connect temperature sensors to inputs 1 and 2.
- Run *Sensing Science Primary* software, selecting two Bar and two Number displays.
- Set the second Bar display and second Number display to show the values from the sensor in input 2.
- Undertake a whole-class demonstration and discussion before letting pairs of pupils test their hands.

▼ Suggested activities

- Two pupils each hold a temperature sensor tightly.
- Watch the changes on each display.
- See what happens if one pupil rubs the tip of the sensor between their fingers.

▼ Assessment focus

- From which display is it easier to see the result?
- Whose hand is warmer?
- What must be decided in order to make it a fair test?
- What happens if you rub the tip of the sensor?

YEAR 4 / P5

Creating a Spreadsheet to Calculate Values ▼

Learning objectives ▼

Pupils learn to:
- use a spreadsheet with built-in calculations;
- enter data into a grid;
- print out the sheet.

ICT resources ▼

A simple spreadsheet program such as *Granada Spreadsheet* (Granada Learning); a sheet set up with headings and cells with formulae included. The formula for each cell in the D column should be C3–B3 (for D3), C4–B4 (for D4) etc.

Vocabulary ▼

calculate
formula
cell

▼ Introduction

- Remind pupils that a spreadsheet is a program that can perform calculations on the data they enter.
- Discuss with the class how they could test fabrics to find the best one for mopping up water spills. Include how they might measure the amount of water soaked up and how to make the investigation fair.

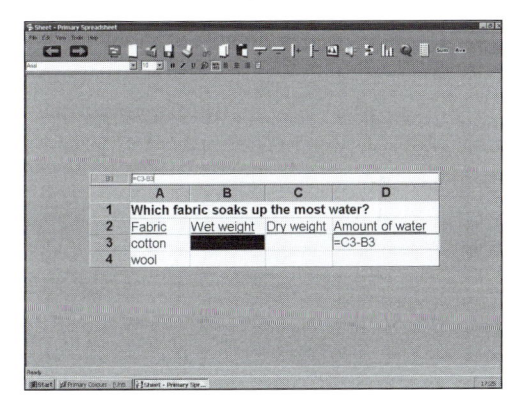

▼ Suggested activities

Pupils:

- cut up different fabrics into pieces the same size and weigh them before and after mopping up the same amount of water;
- enter their results into the spreadsheet grid, which will do the maths for them, working out the amount of water soaked up;
- can draw a bar chart to compare the different fabrics once all the data is entered. A sorted table will produce an ordered list.

▼ Assessment focus

- How can you measure the amount of water soaked up?
- How can you make it a fair test?
- How does the spreadsheet calculate the amount?

Controlling a Floor Robot ▼

Learning objectives ▼

Pupils learn to:
- recognise other applications of control systems;
- put together instructions in sequence to carry out more complicated tasks;
- use repeated instructions.

ICT resources ▼

A floor robot such as Roamer (Valiant Technology) or PIP (Swallow Systems)

Vocabulary ▼

entering instructions and data
creating a sequence of instructions
robot
program

▼ Introduction

- Encourage pupils to recognise that a floor robot is not alive but can only follow instructions. Make the robot travel to a marked area and then follow a simple course to a target, using commands such as Forward, Back, Left, Right etc. Demonstrate how to clear the memory before providing new instructions.
- Practise getting the robot to a particular spot using the fewest possible instructions. Encourage pupils to make predictions of how many will be needed.
- Take account of the effects of friction on the progress of the robot.

▼ Suggested activities

- Demonstrate how to enter a sequence of instructions to make the robot 'draw' simple shapes.
- Discuss how to reduce the number of instructions by using the REPEAT command. For a square, for example, REPEAT four times the sequence of instructions for making one side. Give the pupils a set of three repeated instructions to try out.
- Show pupils how to apply the REPEAT command to make other regular shapes such as equilateral triangles or hexagons. Depending on the time available, you may have to tell them the angle of turn.
- Try the floor robot on different floor surfaces.

▼ Assessment focus

Pupils should:
- recognise that robots follow instructions blindly and cannot think for themselves;
- try to predict the correct instruction and the path that will be followed and test this by programming the floor robot;
- learn that repeated instructions are more efficient and time-saving than long lists of commands.
- learn that friction has an effect on the robot's progress, especially in turning.

YEAR 4 / P5

Modelling Software: Simple Circuits ▼

Learning objectives ▼

Pupils learn to:
- manipulate images and icons;
- make predictions and test them;
- explore aspects of simple circuits and play with variables;
- revise and extend their learning.

ICT resources ▼

Simulation software such as *Simple Circuits* (Soft Teach Educational)

Vocabulary ▼

simulation software

▼ Introduction

- In a whole-class lesson, introduce the software to the pupils. Emphasise that you want them to explore the range of activities and tell them to use their knowledge of circuits gained in science. Similarly, stress the importance of making a prediction and testing it on-screen with the software.

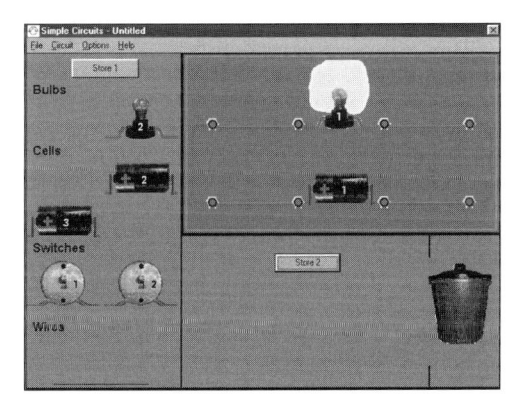

▼ Suggested activities

Pupils:
- work in pairs through the simulation;
- complete one of the varied worksheets provided with the software to show what they have learnt.

▼ Assessment focus

Pupils should:
- recognise that modelling software such as simulations is limited to what the author has included;
- test their ideas and gain further insight into how electricity works in a simple circuit;
- be encouraged to question the results of what they do.

About Ourselves: a Database Project ▼

Learning objectives ▼

Pupils learn to:
- plan the structure of a database by deciding on the information they want to find;
- decide on the fields (headings) under which the data will be entered and design a data-capture form (input screen);
- enter and edit information on the database;
- interrogate the database and print graphs.

ICT resources ▼

A database program such as: *Junior Pinpoint* (Logotron), *Granada Database* (Granada Learning), or *BodyMapper* (TAG Learning)

Vocabulary ▼

database
data file
record
field (heading)

▼ Introduction

- In a whole-class lesson, introduce the software to the pupils using one of the sample data files included.
- Show how a data-capture form can be set up on screen and printed out.
- Discuss which headings might be important. Do not exceed seven or eight for this age group. The following list is suggested: name; birth date; boy or girl; height; hair colour; eye colour; shoe size; run time; pulse rate 1 (at rest); pulse rate 2 (after the run)

▼ Suggested activities

- When the data-capture forms have been photocopied the class can begin entering their personal data.
- Once this has been accomplished, pupils can enter their data into the database in pairs (one types, one checks!).
- After data is entered into the computer it can be sorted into various orders – tallest to shortest etc. Data can be graphed in various ways: a pie chart to show hair colour; a bar chart for heights; and a scatter graph to show whether taller people have bigger feet or whether people with smaller feet have slower run times etc.

Various searches can be undertaken, for example a straight search to locate all those with blonde hair, or a search involving AND (black hair AND brown eyes). This work lays the foundation for future database activities.

▼ Assessment focus

- A database is a collection of records which stores information under specific headings called fields.
- The accuracy of information entered is paramount.
- Information in a database can be sorted, searched, graphed and printed out.

YEAR 5 / P6

Multimedia Presentation

Learning objectives

Pupils learn to:
- create a multimedia presentation using text; retrieved, created and grabbed images; and sounds;
- create links between pages;
- be sensitive to the needs of their audience;
- apply what they have learnt when drawing diagrams in science.

ICT resources

Multimedia authoring software such as *TextEase Studio* (Softease) or *Granada Toolkit* (Granada Learning), a microphone (sound card too if not already fitted), sources of images: ideally a scanner and/or digital camera

Vocabulary

multimedia program
interactive
sound samples
links
buttons
menu

▼ Introduction

- Choose a multimedia CD-ROM to use as an example with the pupils. Good examples exist in CD-ROM encyclopedias and reference materials and in websites on the Internet.
- In a whole-class lesson, set the scene by discussing the differences between books, video and a CD.
- Demonstrate:
  - how to record (sample) sounds and how to create a button to play those sounds;
  - how buttons can create links between pages;
  - a variety of page designs and discuss how emphasis and location are used to help the user understand the page.
- Ask the pupils to evaluate a CD or website.

▼ Suggested activities

- Prepare a set of A4 pages showing sample pages without links, including menu pages and cases where there might be a choice of two pages following on.
- Ask the pupils to work in groups to identify links between the pages, number the pages, draw on any necessary buttons, and write next to them the page each links to.
- Get each group to create a flow-chart type of diagram showing the links between pages, with each arrow labelled with the choice that would appear on screen.
- Get each group to construct their own presentation on any life cycles topic using the computer.

▼ Assessment focus

Pupils should:
- know and recognise how computer programs use sounds, words and images to convey meaning.
- begin to recognise some of the conventions used in computer programs to present information.

YEAR 5 / P6

Finding and Using Information from a CD-ROM (or the Internet) ▼

Learning objectives ▼

Pupils learn to:
- in order to get the information you want you must search the CD-ROM (Internet);
- information stored electronically can be saved for their own use;
- the information is not theirs but the copyright owner's;
- sources of information should be clearly noted.

ICT resources ▼

A CD-ROM encyclopedia, Internet access

Vocabulary ▼

CD-ROM
searching
editing
cut and paste
font size
image size

▼ Introduction

- Confirm that the content of the CD contains information about gases.
- Introduce the CD in a whole-class lesson, demonstrating that the wealth of information can lead to being 'lost'.
- Show how to get a piece of information about an unrelated topic using the search facility.
- Show how to save the information, emphasising that the saved material is for reference only.
- Quit the CD and load DTP software, importing the information. Show the class how to use the software to originate their own text about their research topic.

▼ Suggested activities

Pupils:
- search the CD (in pairs) to find information about gases;
- save information and any illustrations;
- use DTP software to compile their own presentations on gases, using their search results for reference;
- use completed presentations as part of a science display in the classroom.

▼ Assessment focus

- Why should you not copy and edit the saved information?
- How do CD-ROMs and printed encyclopedias compare?
- Do you know the meaning of…? What is a more simple way to say…?
- How will you make your presentation attractive?
- Which font(s) suit(s) this piece?
- Where will you place the picture and the text?

YEAR 5 / P6

Monitoring Temperature: Why Put Salt and Sand on the Roads in Winter? ▼

Learning objectives ▼

Pupils learn that:
- the addition of salt and sand affects melting ice;
- data can be recorded at intervals over a given period of time.

ICT resources ▼

EcoLog and *Sensing Science Primary* software (both Data Harvest) or equivalent monitoring system; two separate temperature sensors

Vocabulary ▼

temperature probe
monitoring
graph plot

▼ Introduction

- This activity explores monitoring temperatures over time using the data-logger.
- As a whole-class activity including pupil interaction, discuss road gritting in winter.
- Make sure that the EcoLog is connected to the computer and switched on. Although Ecolog has a built-in temperature sensor, you will need to use the two probes in the optional sensors pack.
- Run the *Sensing Science Graph Plus* software. Use the setup wizard to select a timespan e.g. 15–25 minutes.
- When completed, look at the pattern of the graph and discuss what has happened.
- A pupil can print out the graph to display in the science corner.

▼ Suggested activities

- Get two cups of crushed ice and place a temperature probe in each cup.
- Add equal amounts of sand and salt to the two cups, sand in one, salt in the other.
- Begin recording the temperature by clicking on the START button at the top of the screen.
- Instead of looking at the graph on screen, watch the values at the top of the screen.
- Continue with other related work while the investigation proceeds. Check the cups periodically to see whether all the ice has melted.

▼ Assessment focus

- What makes ice melt?
- Does the salt or the sand melt the ice?
- Does the ice melt faster in one cup than in the other?
- Is there any difference in temperature between the two cups?

YEAR 5 / P6

Interrogating a Database: How do the Planets Compare? ▼

Learning objectives ▼

Pupils learn:
- that information and data can be obtained from a database;
- how to search for required information efficiently;
- that there are many patterns in the data on the planets.

ICT resources ▼

A datafile containing planetary information created by the teacher or pupils

Vocabulary ▼

search
data
data file
record

▼ Introduction

- Set up a data file with appropriate fields (headings) e.g. name, diameter, rotation, surface temperature, relative gravity, number of moons, atmosphere, distance from the sun etc.
- Enter the data using an encyclopedia for reference and include digital images if possible.
- In a whole-class lesson, introduce the software to the pupils. Emphasise that you want them to search the database to find out answers to certain questions (these can be presented on a worksheet).

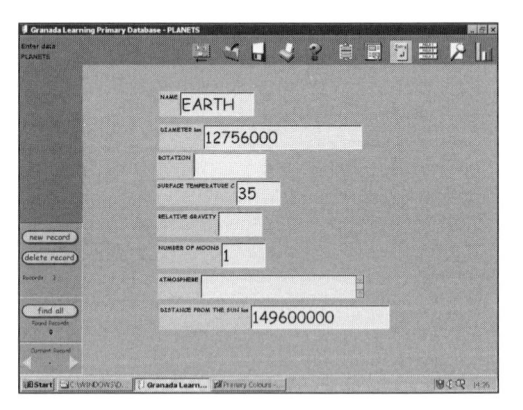

▼ Suggested activities

- Pupils work through the worksheet in pairs, searching the database and recording their answers.
- When all the pupils have completed the activity, gather them together and discuss their findings.

▼ Assessment focus

- Is there a pattern in the sizes of planets and their distances from the sun?
- Do larger planets have more moons?
- Is there a pattern in planets' temperatures and their distances from the sun?
- Can you explain why a (certain pattern) occurs?

YEAR 5 / P6

Exploring Sound ▼

Learning objectives ▼

Pupils learn that:
- the sensor responds quickly to changes in sound;
- the sensor responds to a level of sound and gives a reading;
- there is a measurable difference between loud and quiet sounds.

ICT resources ▼

EcoLog and *Sensing Science Primary* software (both Data Harvest) or equivalent monitoring system; a separate sound sensor
Learning resources: a variety of percussion instruments

Vocabulary ▼

sound sensor

▼ Introduction

- A sound sensor is a very good model of the ear. It has a membrane (diaphragm) which vibrates, sending a signal through wires (nerves) to the computer (brain).
- Make sure that the EcoLog is connected to the computer and switched on. Although EcoLog has a built-in sound sensor, you may wish to use an external sensor as this will emphasise what is happening.
- This activity explores the use of the sound sensor using the *Sensing Science Primary* screens. Review these and what they display. Select Bar, Gauge, Change and Number to make four screen displays.
- Discuss the differences between sound and noise.

▼ Suggested activities

- Make sounds with different objects.
- Watch the changes in the different display screens.
- Try predicting the sound 'shape' a particular instrument may make and test it to check.

▼ Assessment focus

- What happens to:
  - the change screen when there is a loud sound?;
  - the bar when you make different sounds?;
  - the dial when you make different sounds?
- Which display shows the changes best?
- Does the computer remember which was the loudest or quietest sound?
- What difference does distance make to the sound level?
- Does the sound sensor display a reading if you make a sound from behind it?

YEAR 5 / P6

Data-logging: How do Animals Keep Warm? ▼

Learning objectives ▼

Pupils learn that:
- a large animal stays warmer in cold weather than a small animal;
- some animals huddle together in groups to keep warm.

ICT resources ▼

EcoLog and *Sensing Science Primary* software (both Data Harvest) or equivalent monitoring system; two separate temperature sensors
Learning resources: a large plastic bottle, a small plastic bottle, seven empty cans covered in 'fur'

Vocabulary ▼

temperature probe
monitoring
graph plot

▼ Introduction

- This activity explores monitoring temperatures over time using the data-logger.
- Whole-class activity including discussion and pupil interaction. Discuss various ways animals in cold climates keep warm.
- Make sure that the EcoLog is connected to the computer and switched on. Although EcoLog has a built-in temperature sensor, you will need to use the two probes in the optional sensors pack.
- Run the *Sensing Science Graph Plus* software. Use the setup wizard to select a timespan e.g. 15–25 minutes for each activity.

▼ Suggested activities

There are two separate investigations here:

a. Fill the two bottles with water at the same temperature. (Do this in a basin of hot water and leave both in the water until they are at the same temperature.)

- Start the *Sensing Science Graph Plus* software.
- Place the two bottles on a tray and dry their outsides with a cloth. Place the temperature probes in each bottle and begin logging.
- When complete, look at the pattern of the graph and discuss what has happened.
- Pupils can print out the graph to put on display.

b. Fill the seven 'fur'-covered cans with hot water.

- Start the *Sensing Science Graph Plus* software.
- Place six of the cans in a group, with the temperature probe in the central one and the other five cans surrounding it. Place the other probe in a solitary can standing apart from the others.
- When complete, look at the pattern of the graph and discuss what has happened.
- Pupils can print out the graph to accompany their written record.

YEAR 6 / P7

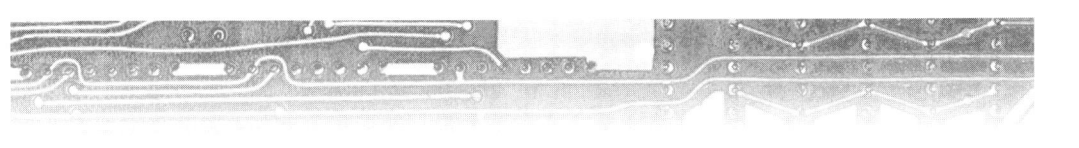

▼ Assessment focus

Activity (a):

- Did one animal cool down more quickly than the other?
- Which animal stayed warmer?
- What would happen if the animals were wet? (This could lead to a similar investigation.)

Activity (b):

- Which animal cooled down quickest?
- How did the group help the central one?
- Which of the cans in the group do you think cooled down more quickly than the central one? (This could lead to a similar investigation.)
- What do you think animals such as penguins do to make sure that the outer members of the huddle don't freeze to death?
- How does fur help an animal?
- Does fur still work well when it is wet? (Again, this could lead to another investigation.)

YEAR 6 / P7

Finding and Using Information from a CD-ROM (or the Internet) ▼

Learning objectives ▼

Pupils learn that:
- in order to get the information you want you must search the CD/Internet;
- information stored electronically can be saved for their own use;
- the information is not theirs but the copyright holder's;
- sources of information should be clearly noted.

ICT resources ▼

A CD-ROM encyclopedia; Internet access

Vocabulary ▼

CD-ROM
searching
editing
cut and paste
font size
image size

▼ Introduction

- Confirm that the content of the CD contains information on micro-organisms.
- Introduce the CD in a whole-class lesson, demonstrating that the wealth of information can lead to being 'lost'.
- Show how to get a piece of information about an unrelated topic using the search facility.
- Show how to save the information, emphasising that the saved material is for reference only.
- Quit the CD and load DTP software, importing the information. Show the class how to use the software to originate their own text about their research topic.

▼ Suggested activities

Pupils:
- search the CD (in pairs) to find information about micro-organisms;
- save information and any illustrations;
- use DTP software to compile their own presentations on micro-organisms, using their search results for reference;
- use completed presentations as part of a science display in the classroom.

▼ Assessment focus

- Why should you not copy and edit the saved information?
- How do CD-ROMs and printed encyclopedias compare?
- Do you know the meaning of . . . ? What is a more simple way to say . . . ?
- How will you make your presentation attractive?
- Which font(s) suit(s) this piece?
- Where will you place the picture and the text?

YEAR 6 / P7

Graphing Information ▼

Learning objectives ▼

Pupils learn:
- that spreadsheets can be used for quickly producing a range of graphs;
- to enter data into a grid;
- to print out a graph;
- to begin to identify an appropriate type of graph for the recorded data.

ICT resources ▼

Spreadsheet software such as *Granada Spreadsheet* (Granada Learning); preferably a colour printer

Vocabulary ▼

spreadsheet
plot
page setup

▼ Introduction

The dissolving of substances, solubility (their ability to dissolve) and solutions (the results of their dissolving) are concepts which can be directly related to pupils' own experiences. Most will have wondered where the sugar goes when it is put into a cup of tea, or watched fascinated at the patterns formed as blackcurrant juice mixes with water. This area of work will involve the pupils collecting data and interpreting it, which lends itself to the use of data-handling ICT tools such as the spreadsheet.

- Talk about sugar in tea or coffee, allowing pupils to put forward their ideas about dissolving.
- Decide which things (variables) can and cannot be tested, through discussion.
- Pupils draw up a list of variables– type of sugar, hot or cold, stirring or not stirring, more or less water, different liquids, different containers.
- They should plan how to record their results in tables and graphs.

▼ Suggested activities

Demonstrate the spreadsheet's graph-creating feature on the computer to a group or the class. As the first groups complete their experiments to relate to curricula guidelines, the teacher or an adult will probably need to help them with inputting their data. (If working in groups, word and interest will quickly spread through the class.)

The important aspect is that they are able to go back to their original hypotheses and confirm whether or not their ideas are correct.

▼ Assessment focus

- Which type of graph is appropriate for this data?
- Does the graph printout confirm whether or not their ideas were correct?

YEAR 6 / P7

Creating a Spreadsheet to Calculate Averages ▼

Learning objectives ▼

Pupils learn to:
- use a spreadsheet with built-in calculations;
- enter data into a grid;
- print out a graph.

ICT resources ▼

A simple spreadsheet program such as *Granada Spreadsheet* (Granada Learning); a setup sheet with headings and cells with formulae included. The formula for each cell in the E column should be (for example): :(SUM B3,D3)/3 (for E3).

Vocabulary ▼

calculate
formula
cell

▼ Introduction

- Remind pupils that a spreadsheet is a program which can perform calculations on the data they enter.
- Discuss with the class investigating how the amount of oxygen available will influence how long a candle will burn.
- Describe the above spreadsheet and how it 'works', pointing out that entering the results on a spreadsheet will help us to see any pattern.

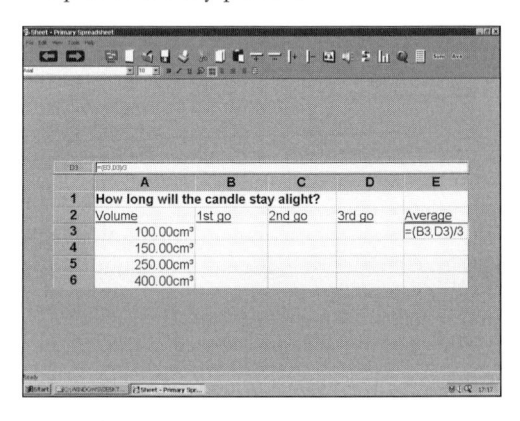

	A	B	C	D	E
1	How long will the candle stay alight?				
2	Volume	1st go	2nd go	3rd go	Average
3	100.00cm³				=(B3,D3)/3
4	150.00cm³				
5	250.00cm³				
6	400.00cm³				

▼ Suggested activities

Pupils:
- can test different sized jars placed over a lighted candle and record the length of time before the candle goes out;
- can record their results on the spreadsheet and use it to draw a bar chart;
- should draw a conclusion from the pattern of results.

▼ Assessment focus

- What does the graph tell you about the different sized jars?
- Why could this be?

YEAR 6 / P7

Blind Spot – Exploring a Website ▼

Learning objectives ▼

Pupils learn to:
- access current data from the Internet;
- navigate through a website;
- use data from the website to investigate a phenomenon.

ICT resources ▼

Internet connected computer(s), printer(s)
Website:
http://serendip.brynmawr.edu/bb/blindspot1.html

Vocabulary ▼

website
URL
logging on

▼ Introduction

Visit the site and look at the range of activities available for investigating blind spots, and adapt the pupils' task(s) according to ability. Sometimes, putting a less able pupil with a more able pupil can prove successful. Bookmark the URL so that pupils will be able to locate it without any typing.

Pupils may need a demonstration of how to proceed in logging on to the Internet and locating the URL.

Create a record sheet for the pupils to record their findings as they undertake the various 'tests'.

▼ Suggested activities

Pupils locate the Blind Spot investigation web pages and work through the tests, recording their results as they go. When all or most of the class have completed the activity, discussion of their results can take place in a plenary session.

Groups could present their results on a chart.

▼ Assessment focus

- Why do we have a blind spot?
- How does colour affect the blind spot?
- How does a line affect the blind spot?
- How does pattern affect the blind spot?

YEAR 6 / P7

Automatic Devices: Control by Computer ▼

Learning objectives ▼

Pupils learn how to:
- control simple devices such as buzzers, motors, bulbs using a basic control box;
- control devices according to a sequence of instructions;
- adjust values in their control program to alter the output;
- make a procedure of their program.

ICT resources ▼

A control box and software such as *Contact Controller* (Data Harvest) including bulbs, buzzers and motors; a number of digital sensors such as a light sensor and a sound sensor
Learning resources: The important outcome is not the technology (building) aspect but the control program the pupils create. Therefore, it may be useful to have a number of models made up for control purposes from Lego Technic® or other construction kits.

Vocabulary ▼

control box
control software
leads
connect
output
words associated with the control program: INPUT etc.
procedure
feedback

▼ Introduction

- Control is a marvellous way for pupils to think about forces or energy.
- Discuss the concept of control using examples such as supermarket doors, barrier gates, radio controlled model cars/boats etc. Discuss the role of the computer: in the door/barrier gates it is making decisions and controlling.
- Show pupils how to plug in all the leads required on the control box and explain that the computer will switch on the buzzer when you give it the correct command. Similarly, it will only switch off the buzzer when given a command (plug the buzzer into output 1).
- Show the pupils the pre-made models (barrier gates, traffic lights etc.) and discuss the possibilities offered by each model.
- If no models are available you may have to focus on designing and making a machine (buggy etc.) in technology prior to introducing computer control.

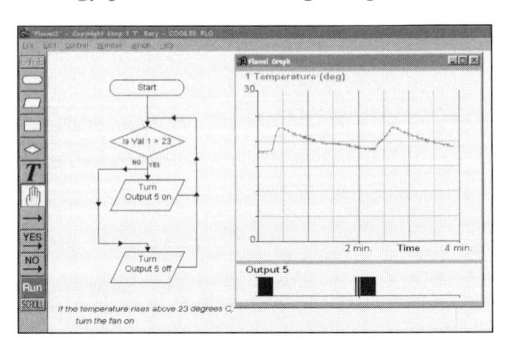

▼ Suggested activities

- Limit the outputs to only one or two devices (a motor or bulb and motor).
- Encourage pupils to develop their control program in simple steps, testing each one as they go.

YEAR 6 / P7

- When each group has developed a satisfactory control program, challenge them to extend it by adding a sensor. For example, with a fan model and a temperature sensor plugged into input 1 on the control box, a control program may look like this:

BUILD FAN
REPEAT
IF INPUT 1 > 24 THEN SWITCH ON 1
IF INPUT 1 < 20 THEN SWITCH OFF 2
AGAIN
END

To run the program type:

RUN FAN

▼ Assessment focus

- Discuss what makes things work 'automatically'.
- It is also important that pupils appreciate why machines and not people do some things: safety, economy and efficiency are the usual reasons.
- Discourage overly ambitious or complicated control programs and emphasise simplicity.

Modelling Software: Simple Circuits ▼

Learning objectives ▼

Pupils learn to:
- manipulate images and icons;
- make predictions and test them;
- explore aspects of simple circuits and play with variables;
- revise and extend their learning.

ICT resources ▼

Simulation software such as *Simple Circuits* (Soft Teach Educational)

Vocabulary ▼

simulation

▼ Introduction

In a whole-class lesson, reintroduce the software to the pupils, reminding them that they used it at a simple level in the earlier activity. Emphasise that you now want them to explore a wider range of activities. The aim is to extend the knowledge of circuits they gained in the earlier activity. Stress the importance of making a prediction and testing it on-screen with the software.

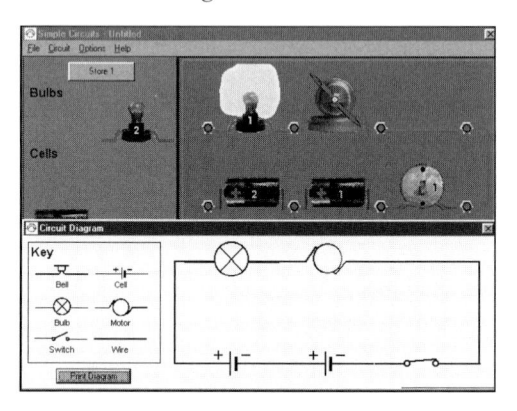

▼ Suggested activities

- Pupils work in pairs through the simulation.
- They complete one of the varied worksheets provided with the software to show what they have learnt.

▼ Assessment focus

Pupils should:
- recognise that modelling software such as simulations is limited to what the author has included;
- test their ideas and gain further insight into how electricity works in a simple circuit;
- be encouraged to question the results of what they do.

YEAR 6 / P7

Measuring Dandelions: Using ICT to Store and Present Data ▼

Learning objectives ▼

Pupils learn to:
- plan the structure of a database by deciding on the information they want to find out.
- decide on the fields (headings) under which the data will be entered.
- design a data capture form (input screen).
- enter and edit information on the database.
- interrogate the database and print graphs.

ICT resources ▼

Database management software such as *Junior Pinpoint* (Logotron), *Granada Database* (Granada Learning) or *TextEase Database* (Softease)
Learning resources: Unit 5/6H of the DfEE QCA Science Scheme of Work (September 2000) which can be accessed via www.standards.dfee.gov.uk/schemes/science/sci5_6h?version=/&view=get

Vocabulary ▼

database
data file
record
field (heading)
entry

▼ Introduction

- In a whole-class lesson, remind the children how to use the software using data files included with the package.
- Brainstorm which headings might be important. The following list is suggested: dandelion number; length of grass 1; length of grass 2; sunny; shady; length of leaf 1; length of leaf 2; flower 1; and flower 2.

▼ Suggested activities

a. On the first visit to the site:
- Work through the survey outlined in Unit 5/6H.
- Pupils measure and enter their data onto their own prepared data capture form.
- On return to the classroom, enter the data into a database.
- Various searches can be undertaken e.g. a straight search to locate dandelions with length of leaf greater than a specified number of cm, or a search involving AND (flower 1 AND shady).
- Data can be graphed in various ways, such as a pie chart to show shady and sunny habitats.

b. On the second visit to the site:
- Gather information for the '2' data fields.
- Carry out further comparisons of the data.

▼ Assessment focus

Pupils understand:
- that a database is a collection of records which stores information under specific headings called fields.
- that information in a database can be sorted, searched, graphed and printed out.
- that information can be graphed to reveal patterns and answer 'if it had...it might...' questions.
- how to use the results to check plausibility, working practices, limitations of the investigation method etc.

YEAR 6 / P7

Glossary

branching database	a hierarchical database
button/icon	a small image or picture representing a command or function
CD-ROM	Compact Disc Read-Only Memory – an external storage medium
cell	a box in a spreadsheet which can hold either data or a formula
click select	clicking the mouse's left-hand button
control	in ICT means using software commands to control a device
control box	a device enabling a computer to control models or external devices
control software	the software required to 'drive' the control box
cut and paste	to move blocks of data around an application
database	a collection of information held in computer-readable form
data file	a collection of records in a database
data-logger	a device for automatically collecting measurements of environmental data
drag	to click on a screen object and move it using the mouse pointer
drop	when dragging an object releasing the left mouse button will drop it
editing	amending and altering data
field	a single heading on a record 'card'
file	data that has been entered and saved with a filename
font	a style of typeface
graphics	computer generated pictures
key system	a system which can locate information
links	'hot spots' on a web page which take you to another page or section or URL
load	to install a program in memory
logging on	gaining access to a network (including the Internet)
menu	a table of choices
modelling	simulation software and spreadsheets
mouse	an input device for selecting objects on the screen
multimedia	combination of text, graphics, sounds, video clips, animations, photos etc.
pointer	the mouse cursor
print	to output text or graphics via a printer
program	a set of instructions to make a computer perform a task or job
record	one component set of information in a database
robot	a device which can be controlled via a program of instructions
run	to start a program in memory
screen or VDU	output device providing the user with feedback from the computer
search	to make the computer go through all or part of the records in its database to find those that correspond to certain criteria
sensor	a device for sensing changes in the environment
simulation	an imitation of a real life activity or scenario on the computer
sort	to put records into an order or into groups, often to be ready for print-out
spreadsheet	a grid which can hold both data and formulae
URL	the unique address of a website
website	a set of web pages belonging to one organisation or person